BIOLOGICAL ESPIONAGE

'This is truly scary stuff ... A thought-provoking work'

Library Journal (USA)

The author in 1985 at the beginning of his career in the KGB

Alexander Kouzminov

BIOLOGICAL ESPIONAGE

*Special Operations of the Soviet and Russian Foreign
Intelligence Services in the West*

With an Introduction by Nigel West

Greenhill Books, London
Stackpole Books, Pennsylvania

Greenhill Books

Biological Espionage
Special Operations of the Soviet and Russian Foreign Intelligence Services in the West

First published in 2005 by Greenhill Books
Lionel Leventhal Ltd, Park House
1 Russell Gardens, London NW11 9NN
and
Stackpole Books
5067 Ritter Road, Mechanicsburg, PA 17055, USA

British Library Cataloguing-in Publication Data

Kouzminov, Alexander
Biological espionage: special operations of the Soviet and Russian foreign intelligence
services in the West
1. Soviet Union. 2. Espionage, Soviet. 3. Espionage, Russian. 4. Bioterrorism – Russia
(Federation)
I. Title
327.1'247

ISBN 1-85367-646-2

Library of Congress Cataloging-in Publication Data available

For more information on our books, please visit www.greenhillbooks.com, email
sales@greenhillbooks.com, or telephone us within the UK on 020 8458 6314.
You can also write to us at the above London address.

Edited by Owen Lock
Maps drawn by Derek Stone
Typeset by GCS, Leighton Buzzard, Bedfordshire, LU7 1AR
Printed and bound by CPD (Wales), Ebbw Vale

Contents

Maps

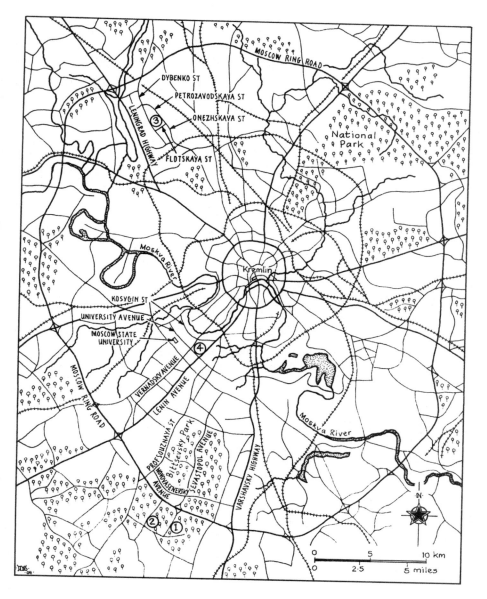

General Map of Moscow

1. KGB First Chief Directorate (now SVR) Headquarters. 2. Guarded residences for senior officers and the most valuable Illegals. 3. Andropov Red Banner Intelligence Institute (advanced-training faculty). 4. Dept 12 conspiracy apartment, codename GVOZDIKA

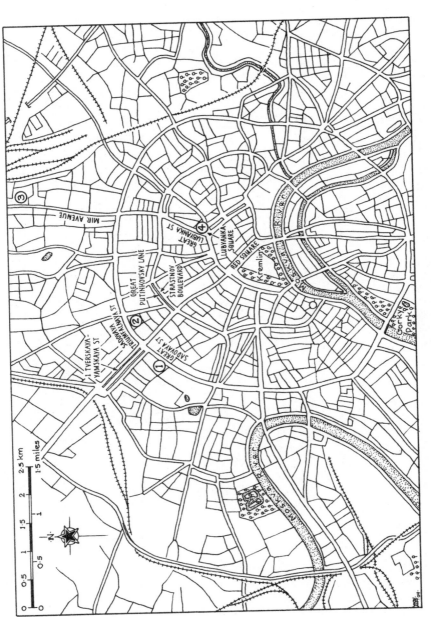

Central Moscow

1. Dept 12 conspiracy apartment where the author liaised with the Fedorovs. 2. Dept 12 conspiracy apartment where the author first met Colonel Yuri Shcherbakov in 1984. 3. Dept 3 conspiracy apartment for the training of Illegals. 4. KGB (now FSB) Headquarters

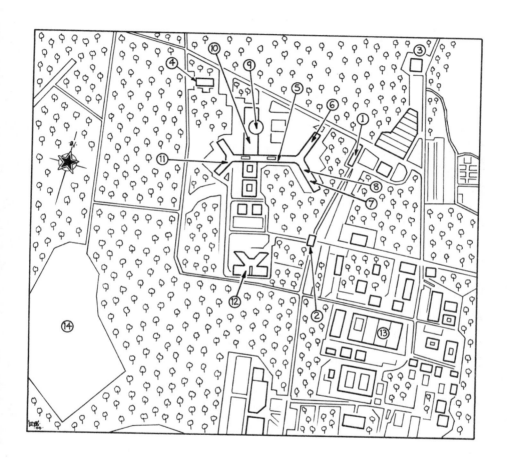

KGB First Chief Directorate (now SVR) Headquarters
(see 1 on General Map of Moscow)

1. Main entrance. 2. Guarded entrance. 3. Checkpoint. 4. Reserve entrance. 5. Main building. 6. Offices of the director and his deputies. 7. SVR archives and library. 8. Cryptography department. 9. Conference hall. 10. Foreign-languages-training department. 11. Directorate S. 12. The NIIRP. 13. Technical auxiliary services. 14. Guarded residences (see 2 on General Map of Moscow)

Introduction

Biological Espionage represents an important and unique breakthrough, shedding light for the first time on the hitherto unsuspected operations of a branch within the KGB's famed Directorate S that has survived into the present times within the modern Russian Foreign Intelligence Service.

Following the collapse of the Soviet Bloc the West's intelligence agencies were inundated with offers from KGB retirees to disclose information that they hoped would be considered valuable. One joke circulating was that there were so many volunteers seeking a new life in the capitalist world that prospective defectors were invited to form orderly queues outside embassies. Few of these individuals achieved any publicity, apart from Vasili Mitrokhin, who was to achieve worldwide fame for the extraordinary collection of documents he had copied while serving as the KGB First Chief Directorate's archivist over several decades. Mitrokhin, who died in England in 2004, revealed unprecedented quantities of information, especially about Directorate S of the First Chief Directorate, an organisation previously shrouded in mystery because of the extreme levels of secrecy necessarily associated with Illegal operations.

Whatever the organisation, the work of personnel deployed abroad without the benefit of diplomatic immunity will always make them the most vulnerable. Thus the CIA's programme of infiltrating professionals under 'non-official cover' into target countries remains the holiest of holies within the elite Directorate of Operations, and its counterparts in other countries, including France and Israel, take elaborate precautions to backstop, protect and support their officers who undertake these exceptionally hazardous duties, very often in 'denied territories' where they are most likely to be at serious risk.

Directorate S had long been admired for the impressive quality of its training and the dedication of its staff, who during the Cold War spent many years overseas burrowing into their host communities, deflecting suspicion, and experiencing considerable personal privations to achieve their objectives. Their loyalty was rewarded; in the cases of Willie Fisher and Konon Molody, two Illegal *rezidents* arrested and sentenced to long terms of imprisonment in the United States and Britain respectively, both were freed in spy-swaps negotiated to obtain their freedom. Within the First Chief Directorate, Illegals attained a special status, and deservedly so.

The work of the Illegal is universally recognised as quite the most dangerous in a field hardly considered risk-free at the best of times, and therefore it is not surprising that very little has been published about this extremely specialised area of intelligence collection. However, even within the innermost sanctums of Directorate S, there was a section, the very existence of which was a closely held secret rarely shared with other insiders. This was Department 12, curiously absent from the conventional wiring diagrams developed by Western analysts who had seized hungrily on any crumb concerning Directorate S that filtered through to London or Washington DC. Throughout the entire Cold War, among all the KGB defectors who sought asylum in Britain and the United States, only Vladimir Kuzichkin had worked for Directorate S, as an Illegals support officer, so the West's knowledge of this particularly arcane field was necessarily limited. Others, such as Oleg Gordievsky, who had been occasionally co-opted to undertake Illegal support duties at the London *rezidentura*, and whose brother had trained as an Illegal, served to shed some light on the subject, but generally those counter-intelligence experts who studied this rarified subject found themselves working largely in the dark, eager for any clue to study.

This, then, is the remarkable background to Alexander Kouzminov's unique account of his ten years in Directorate S, and his decision to describe his work as an intelligence officer and Doctor of Biological Sciences tasked to acquire information about the WMD capabilities researched by potential adversaries. He is no whistleblower in the mould of Ken Alibek, the microbiologist who defected in 1992 and denounced the Kremlin for officially sponsored, wholesale breaches of the Biological Weapons Convention; rather, Kouzminov is a back-room boffin seeking to compile realistic assessments of the research projects underway in other countries. Not for him the development of lethal pathogens in a sealed laboratory – instead the skilled insertion of highly trained and dedicated Illegals into some of the most secure environments on the globe. Nor was this some irrelevant academic exercise to monitor research that was never likely to be weaponised or tailored into a warhead. Indeed, in a post-Gulf War era, when the proliferation of chemical and biological weapons is a major preoccupation for the democracies, posing arguably the most serious threat to regional, if not global, economic and political stability, there can hardly be a topic more engaging for intelligence collectors or their political masters.

In the British and American context, the failure of the Iraq Survey Group to find Saddam's much-vaunted secret laboratories, or his stockpiles of WMD, highlights the weaknesses of conventional collection methods, especially when compared to the successes achieved by the less orthodox techniques practised by Directorate S and described in this book. Sophisticated overhead-reconnaissance platforms, signals-interception programmes, and procurement monitoring turned out to have been of little assistance in the coalition's efforts to scrutinise forensically Baghdad's universally acknowledged overt commitment to the development of WMD. What made the boasts about bunkers filled with anthrax so chilling was the certainty that Saddam had not only used chemical weapons on his own people, but had declared his intent to construct and deploy a viable nuclear device during Desert Storm. No amount of gossip-laden defectors from the regime, among them even members of Saddam's immediate family, proved to be a substitute for the recruitment of knowledgeable informants with direct, first-hand access to the sites creating and storing WMD. It is now known, from the evidence published in Lord Butler's review of WMD intelligence, that although Iraq had been regarded as a key collection target for more than a quarter of a century, Britain's Secret Intelligence Service had only managed to recruit five sources in Baghdad. Of those five, one did not have any direct knowledge but simply relayed the gist of conversations he overheard, the two main sources were unreliable, and the remaining pair turned out to be sub-sources of the agents whose reports had been discredited.

Foreign liaison agencies appear to have fared no better, with their reporting having become increasingly dependent on politically motivated émigré opposition groups who were anxious to exaggerate, if not invent, the scale of the threat presented by Saddam's despotic regime. In other words, after years of opportunity, SIS's case officers had fallen into the grasp of fabricators, hoaxers and purveyors of deception, and attempts to verify information through liaison channels had been doomed. SIS's famed CX product, the top-secret designation of the agency's classified reporting, given very limited circulation in Whitehall, proved to be fundamentally flawed, thus leaving the supposedly independent analysts to draw up assessments based on a paucity of material that at best was unreliable, and at worst had been embroidered.

But how could such a fiasco happen? SIS had been quick to blame post-Cold War starvation of resources by budget-cutting politicians who had forced the organisation to abandon the tried-and-tested separation of collection and requirements. Inexperienced desk officers had been assigned collection tasks, thus robbing them of the discipline imposed by the conventional divide between requirements and production. Thus SIS, prompted by financial considerations and the introduction of personal incentives based on results, had undermined the foundations of orthodox intelligence collection that had taken more than ninety years to perfect.

Having established how *not* to penetrate a target, can Directorate S offer a model of what could have been achieved? Evidently the Soviet Union regarded no Western establishment, however well protected, as completely immune from the attention of Illegals, and we learn that during the Cold War both Porton Down and Fort Detrick were the subject of sustained, concentrated attention from well-qualified personnel who had been directed to insinuate themselves into their assigned premises. This is human intelligence at its most effective, insulated from the occupational hazards of second-rate recruiters pitching third-rate fabricators who could never hope to pass a polygraph test, and seem to exist only to peddle bogus material on unsuspecting, grateful recipients who are devoid of corroboration.

Human intelligence, so often presented as a more reliable channel of accurate reporting than high-tech, high-flying reconnaissance aircraft, unmanned drones, and signals-intelligence satellites, is actually a messy business requiring case officers to cultivate, recruit and run people who are willing to sell out their countries, governments or even families. As Kouzminov notes, huge investment in time and money is required

> to train, place and settle successfully just one Illegal overseas. Training alone normally takes five to seven years: learning at least two foreign languages, one of which is polished to perfection as the Illegal's mother tongue; operational and intelligence training; studying precise details of the country where the Illegal is to live and work; and many other things. Typically, only a few individuals from among the hundreds selected by Department 3 successfully finished their training.

The human source is someone with shifting loyalties, unpredictable appetites, and dubious motives who may require constant integrity testing to ensure he (or she) has not adopted an independent agenda. Such individuals are not graduates of the Mother Theresa school of intelligence gathering, but complex, dynamic personalities, occasionally sociopathic, who require, and maybe demand, delicate handling. Every recruited source is a potential double agent transformed, perhaps overnight, from a trusted, reliable source into manipulative monomaniac. In much the same way that over-reliance on technology can leave an assessment structure vulnerable to co-ordinated deception, human intelligence is even more susceptible to the foibles that make the task of the agent-handler so challenging. This is nothing to do with developing language ability, acquiring the ethnic invisibility to melt unnoticed into the souk, or undertaking clandestine surveillance in the bazaar. It is far more about the interpersonal skills required to build the relationships that successful case officers share with their agents, engendering mutual trust, loyalty and dependability.

Of course, novelists have preferred to portray dedicated intelligence professionals, as John Bingham complained to John le Carré, as 'moles, morons, shits and homosexuals', a description that he pointed out to his former protégé 'makes the intelligence job no easier'. Where loyalties are divided, either on religious or ideological lines, the absolutes in a traditionally murky world are easier to discern; but what happens in the more complicated, real world where black and white is traded for shades of grey, and spin is substituted for truths? In such uncertain environments the Illegal is an attractive, dependable asset, albeit one that may have required years of heavy investment. The concept of the mole dates back to Francis Bacon in 1682, and endless patience is required to allow an Illegal to build a plausible legend, transit through third countries before reaching the one of their destination, and then achieve the desired position which allows the required access. However, in a computer-driven climate where politicians facing re-election will settle for nothing less than instant remedies, endless patience may be a commodity in short supply. In the Soviet example, where such democratic imperatives were never considerations, the intelligence machine could invest long-term and farm for a future dividend that may have seemed far off, but nonetheless certain. Thus the recruits of the 'great Illegals' of the 1930s were still active thirty years later, Kim Philby and Anthony Blunt being good examples. They had been pitched soon after graduating from Cambridge, but survived respectively until January 1963, when Philby defected to Moscow, and April 1964, when Sir Anthony Blunt accepted an immunity from prosecution in return for his confession.

Today's world of international terrorism, cyber-crime and identity theft is a far cry from the reassuring, apparently permanent state of balanced super-power confrontation that gave the world relative stability for more than half a century after the defeat of Nazi Germany. Nuclear stalemate and the principle of deterrence, based on mutually assured destruction, has no relevance in an era of suicide bombings, undisguised genocide, political extremism, ethnic cleansing, and atrocities committed by religious zealots. Can such modern plagues be contained by the application of classic counter-intelligence orthodoxy? Only by understanding precisely what has happened in the past can sound judgements be made about how current vicissitudes should be addressed. To learn how Department 12 of Directorate S tackled quite the most challenging adversaries can be an advantage.

NIGEL WEST

Editor's Note

Alexander Kouzminov is a professional in the fields of espionage and microbiology. Now a Russian émigré, he happened to live through interesting times in the Soviet Union and was long an officer within the most secret division of the Soviet and Russian external intelligence services, what used to be called the Illegals Directorate. His is a cautionary tale, told with the detail available only to someone who lived the story. Frank details about the most sensitive areas of the KGB are rare even today, when the floodgates of Russian publishing have opened to unleash upon the world a very large body of water indeed. It is not always the clearest, and frequently it needs to be filtered so the essence of what is floating about within it may be made visible, but it is quite a great volume.

In 1962, unable to live with the consequences of a decision to major in physics at college, I dropped out midway through my first year and joined the air force. There I spent a very intensive year being taught Russian at Syracuse University and a further two lumbering along the borders of the Soviet Union in C-130s, trolling for unguarded radio conversations among the officers of Soviet anti-aircraft missile sites. There were many, and the work was fascinating, but eventually I decided to return to college, where I majored in Russian literature. After graduation, I became a supervisor of translations from the Russian at Plenum Press, a 'scientific and technical' publishing house in New York City, before chancing across a position at Random House.

In the course of a twenty-five year career at Random House, I edited general fiction and non-fiction, science fiction, military memoirs, translations from the Russian and from the classical Chinese, and more than thirty non-fiction works devoted to the subject of espionage. My favourites by far were, in no particular order, the translations, the military memoirs, and those works on espionage.

My interest in that last field had been excited when, as a child in the early 1950s, I watched the televised unveiling of the mystery around Nikolai Khokhlov, an officer of the KGB who had been despatched to West Germany to direct an assassination team targeted against a man whose existence the Soviet government found inconvenient. Over the years I tracked down and interviewed various of the principals in that drama, read Khokhlov's interesting English-language memoir, and spoke with by then Professor Khokhlov himself at length about his experiences. It was he who introduced me to what was then the very best book written by an insider on the subject of work within the KGB, *The Right to a Conscience* [*Pravo Na Sovest*], his own Russian-language memoir that was directed specifically at the Soviet audience and which was smuggled into the Soviet Union by the CIA. Twice as long as its English-language counterpart, *The Right to a Conscience* was full to overflowing with the kind of technical detail that the editor of Dr Khokhlov's English-language memoir had deleted as she thought it uninteresting. *The Right to a Conscience* remained the stand-out book in its field until it was joined nearly four decades later by Pavel Sudoplatov's *Special Tasks*. Sudoplatov had been Khokhlov's boss within the KGB, and his revelations placed Khoklov's in their full context.

One looks in vain for new works with the startling frankness of the memoirs of Khokhlov and Sudoplatov; even today, one finds more often descriptions of bloody great thugs that could easily pass for hagiography rather than for history. Still, much of use to historians is being published and, despite backsliding under Putin, we may look forward to more. One hopes one or two will be as interesting and important as the volume in the reader's hand. In today's Russia it could not be published.

In 2005, Khokhlov and Sudoplatov have met their match: they spoke mostly of their pasts; Kouzminov describes his past, the world's present, and warns of some very disturbing futures. The wise reader will pay him heed.

OWEN LOCK

Author's Note

Ten years have passed since I left the intelligence service. I have lived far away from Russia for eight of those years, keeping silent about my past. But, because of the events of 11 September 2001, and the subsequent potential and quite serious threat of biological terrorism and sabotage around the world, I think the time has come for me to speak out.

This book is about the work of the top secret Department 12 of Directorate S (Special Operations)* – the elite inner core of the former Soviet KGB First Chief Directorate and its successor, the Russian Foreign Intelligence Service,† during the 1980s and early 1990s.

The main tasks of Department 12 were: biological espionage, planning and preparation of acts of biological terrorism and sabotage; carrying them out in the event of a large-scale military conflict or a war between Russia and the West; assisting in the preparation for biological warfare; and supporting the Soviet, later the Russian, biological weapons programme. This was done primarily through the activities of so-called 'Illegals', Russian intelligence operatives who were secretly deployed to the West and covertly operated there under assumed names and well-documented cover stories, masquerading as citizens of Western countries.

---

* Directorate S – Special operations in target countries – is also called the Directorate of Illegal Intelligence.

† The Russian Foreign Intelligence Service (SVR) was created from the First Chief Directorate (Foreign Intelligence) of the Soviet Union's KGB in 1991.

I hope that this book will be of interest not only to the general public, but that it will also attract the attention of intelligence services. I do not intend to push a political line for or against any state and its policies. The events I discuss are really only part of a much wider picture. I do not exclude the possibility that intelligence services of other countries have carried out similar activities. One of the aims of the book is to point out the need for active international co-operation so that the risks that have arisen as a result of international biological espionage activities can be properly managed.

In general, the names of my former colleagues from Department 12, as well as other intelligence officers with whom I had the chance to work, are abbreviated or are not mentioned. This is in order not to harm them, or their families. In addition I have avoided disclosure of the real names of foreign-born secret agents and the Illegals with whom I had to work as part of my duty in Department 12. Only their operational pseudonyms and codenames are mentioned. Some technical details about operations of Department 12 outside Russia have been omitted. Full names are given only for those who have retired or died, i.e. to those for whom these pages pose no threat, whether to career or to freedom. The only officers who are clearly identified by their real names are those who betrayed the Service, suffered a fatal end to their careers, died of natural causes, or can be clearly identified as a result of memoirs they themselves or others have published.

Behind every event, behind every government worker involved in these events, there were spies, although the authors of scientific chronicles – whether it is because of high egos, or feelings of disgust – ignore the spies' input and rarely mention their names. Even those political personas, diplomats, generals and scientists, whom the secret agents gave priceless help, keep quiet about this.

Ladislas Farago
War of Wits

ВЫЧИСЛИТЕЛЬНЫЙ ЦЕНТР ВНИИПИ

СВИДЕТЕЛЬСТВО № **00450**

Настоящее свидетельство выдано гр. _____

К У З Ь М И Н О В У

АЛЕКСАНДРУ ЮРЬЕВИЧУ

в том, что он обучался

с " 5 " _января_ 19 87 г.

по " 5 " _июня_ 19 87 г.

по программе подготовки водителя транспорт-
ных средств категории "В" и на выпускных
экзаменах

согласно протоколу № _0-65_

от " 8 " _июня_ 19 87 г.

получил следующие оценки ("удовлетвори-
тельно", "хорошо", "отлично"):

Устройство, техническое обслуживание и правила технической эксплуатации _хорошо_

Правила дорожного движения _хорошо_

Практическое вождение _зачет_

Руководитель организации _____

Председатель экзаменационной
комиссии _____

Выдано удостоверение серии _ЯБ Б_

№ _514439_

Госавтоинспекцией **гор. МОСКВЫ**

МВД УВД _Мосгорисполкома_

М.П. _июня_ 19 87 г.

подпись

Документ на право управления транспорт-
ным средством не служит

Top: International driving licence, given to the author by the VNIIPI (Computing Centre for All-Union Scientific Research on Industrial Information) when he was in the KGB Andropov Red Banner Intelligence Institute. The VNIIPI was used as a cover organisation for the Intelligence Institute's advanced-training faculty (see 3 on General Map of Moscow). *Below left and right:* Cover registrations in Moscow during the author's training in the Andropov Intelligence Institute and soon after his graduation. These addresses (3-aya Radialnaya Ul., d. 11, kv. 14 (left) and Ul. Menzhinskogo, d. 13, korp. 3, kv. 16 (right)) were used in the 1980s and early 1990s by the intelligence services for many of the institute's cadets and young intelligence operatives. Sometimes dozens of young officers and their families 'lived' simultaneously at the same address, according to their official registrations. Registration, or *propiska*, is compulsory in Russia

Prologue

S cience and intelligence. These, at first glance, distantly separated fields of human activity, are very often closely tied together. Many revolutionary scientific creations were made with the help of intelligence services. Let's say that now it is a fundamental fact that the first Soviet atomic bomb, tested in 1949, was an exact copy of an American one. It is certain that Russian scientists and engineers could have made their own bomb step-by-step even without any help from their intelligence services but, thanks to the information stolen by spies from secret atom laboratories, in Los Alamos and elsewhere, the Soviet bomb was produced within a very short time and without the huge expenditure of money and resources that independent reinvention would have required.

As for biological warfare, both Soviet science and Soviet intelligence started to pay considerable interest to it straight after the 1917 revolution. During the 1920s, Lenin ordered the establishment of a secret 'Laboratory X', which was involved in creating and testing undetectable poisons and toxic biological products. With the help of such powerful and silent weapons, the highest Soviet authority got rid of its enemies – political opponents, dissidents, double agents, and defectors. In 1937 Laboratory X was transferred to the NKVD and from then on was accountable to the Minister of State Security. To carry out secret political assassinations, the resources of the intelligence services were used – Soviet agents and intelligence officers, who were deployed in the West.

In 1936 in Russia, pathogens of anthrax and tularaemia were accepted into the military arsenal. At about the same time the first military exercises were used to work out the method of applying them. These new weapons were successfully used during World War II against the approaching army of the German general Paulus near the city of Rostov.

Laboratory X was subordinated to and supervised by the NKVD Ministry of State Security chiefs, Beria, Abakumov, and Ignatiev. In his memoir *Special Tasks*, General Pavel Sudoplatov – the head of the NKVD's Department of Special Tasks (which carried out the murder of Stalin's political opponents in exile), and Deputy Director of Foreign Intelligence from 1939 to 1942 – wrote that 'at the end of the 1940s to the start of the 1950s, the Soviet intelligence services began to gain more and more information about research activity in the USA and in England dealing with the creation of biological warfare'.

The Soviet Illegals Morris and Leontina Cohen, who operated at the start of the 1940s in the USA and who made a large contribution to Soviet efforts to obtain atomic secrets, were later sent to England, in 1954, where they started to work under new, assumed, names: Peter and Helen Kroger (under the codename DACHNIKI). In England this husband-and-wife agent team was put under control of Gordon Lonsdale, a.k.a. Konon Molody, *rezident* of the KGB Illegal network, or *rezidentura*. Lonsdale was operating under the codename BEN. Until 1961, these Illegals gathered and transferred to the Soviet Union Britain's most valuable secrets about the creation of biological weapons. It is only quite recently that part of their top-secret files, including cipher correspondence with Moscow Centre, have become public.

In January 1961, the DACHNIKI and BEN were arrested in London. In 1969 they were exchanged for three British citizens who had been arrested and spent some years in a Russian prison for alleged espionage. But the DACHNIKI were only one part of the network of Illegals and their equals that had been dispersed into the West by the leadership of Soviet intelligence.

As the Israeli intelligence services have revealed, at the start of the 1950s a Soviet spy, Marcus Klinberg, was a director of one of Israel's secret biological centres. Klinberg passed intelligence information to the Soviet Union about the bacteriological warfare programme of Israel. His activity caused (as the Israeli government itself stated) a significant level of damage to that country's defence system. Actually, it is amazing that a country as new as Israel was in the late 1940s and early 1950s already had its own secret biological weapons programme and that Soviet intelligence already knew about it! In the early 1980s, Klinberg's treason was discovered and he was given a twenty-year jail sentence. The fact of his arrest was kept secret. All this time he was under strict custody. Even though the Soviet government made many offers to swap Klinberg for some of the Soviet Union's well-known Jewish dissidents, Israel's government refused its demands. In 1998 the eighty-four-year-old scientist was freed from prison due to poor health.

But it was only from the beginning of the 1970s that interest in the use of biological weapons for future war started to grow. In 1972, for the first time in human history, scientists 'split' DNA – and genetic engineering was born, that is, it became a possibility to manipulate the genomes of living organisms. Yet at the first international conference on genetic engineering research held in Asilomar, USA, in 1975, it was already noted that recombinant DNA technologies could make significant contributions to the conduct of biological warfare. And the first such genetic experiments immediately attracted the attention of military interests.

As early as 1973, a secret decision of the Soviet Union's Ministry Council decreed that preparations be made for biological warfare on a new basis – with the help of molecular biology and genetic engineering.

After 1973 a civil system to prepare for biolgoical war was created, paralleling the military programme. This was controlled by the KGB and the GRU, and acted according to an order of Directorate 15 of the General Staff of the Ministry of Defence. For additional secrecy this civil part of the biological weapons programme was included in a civil department – the Chief Agency of Microbiological Industry (Glavmikrobioprom) – and was hidden under the general name of a research agency, Biopreparat. Numerous ministries and many scientific research institutes and laboratories, which carried out secret experiments with dangerous pathogens of human and animal diseases, were involved in the programme. All of Biopreperat's institutes had two laboratory groups: one set was more or less public, legitimate, for peaceful research; the other was secret, and it was to create combat strains of micro-organisms. In total there were about forty institutes and factories inside Biopreparat.

Ken Alibek, the former deputy director of this agency, wrote about the scientific part of it in his book *Biohazard*. There he mentions several times a 'mysterious' person – an 'engineer' called Valery Butuzov, 'a tall, gangly fellow in his early forties with a short military haircut', who retreated from closer contact. 'No one understood what he did. Sometimes he disappeared for days at a time.' Alibek remembers that even Biopreparat's deputy head, General Anatoly Vorobyov, who complained about 'lazy' Butuzov all the time, had no power to fire him.

So, who was Butuzov? At first, Alibek says that the main place of Butuzov's work was some surreptitious 'Military Laboratory X', and then he writes that it was a secret pharmacological institute. At the end of his book Alibek again returns to Butuzov, and points out that he in fact 'had worked for many years developing assassination weapons' in 'a Laboratory 12, the unit operated by the KGB First Chief Directorate'.

Alibek is mistaken. Secret Laboratory 12, which belonged to the KGB Scientific-Research Institute for Advanced Technologies (it was known as Laboratory X before 1960), really existed in the heart of Moscow, not far from Lubyanka Square. According to former KGB general Oleg Kalugin, it was shut down in 1970.

In reality, my colleague Valery Butuzov, a career intelligence officer and a colonel who'd been awarded the Red Banner medal for a clandestine combat operation, worked in Department 12 of Directorate S (Special Operations) of the Soviet (later Russian) Foreign Intelligence Service. This was the department responsible for biological espionage (intelligence) and international biological terrorism. I worked in that top-secret intelligence department for almost ten years and was a first-hand witness to the events that are described in this book. I tell about the department's tasks and plans; its new tactics after its 'reformation' in the early 1990s; its clandestine operations in the West; and its personnel, my former colleagues.

Some people might say that we helped with preparations for total biological war and would judge us. Others might say that we assisted in strengthening the balance between the superpowers. In the end, all nations act to protect their own interests. But in this book I am not talking about 'good guys' and 'bad guys' on different sides of the barricades. The creation, perfection, and application of biological weapons has become the most dangerous area of inquiry of mankind, one which can lead to the destruction of all human life. The simplicity and low cost of biological weaponry have attracted the attention of the military, rogue scientists, terrorists, extremist organisations, and aggressive governments. Modern biological weapons are hard to identify and it is almost impossible to prevent their development. Every new generation of such weaponry is more refined. And that refinement progresses with each new development and breakthrough in genetic engineering. The weapon can easily escape the control of its creators. The biological demon must be stopped, and that can only be done through the co-ordinated work of many countries. There is a need for international co-operation to control biological weapons proliferation. This task must become our common goal in the twenty-first century.

Chapter 1

Hot Topic

D ecember, 1984. Outside the windows it is already dusk; Moscow winter days are short. Snow is falling, covering the grounds of the Soviet Intelligence Service Headquarters. There are only a few days until New Year's Eve. The year 1985 will bring many changes – the reformer Gorbachev will come to power, *perestroika* will begin, relations with the West will improve. But in December 1984 'the evil empire', as Ronald Reagan called the Soviet Union, is ruled by the Communist Politburo. It is already the sixth year of our invasion of Afghanistan, which is strongly condemned by the West. In Europe NATO has unwrapped Pershing missiles aimed at Moscow. And in East Germany Soviet cruise-missiles are deployed to destroy European capitals if ordered to do so by the Kremlin. The Cold War is becoming increasingly tense.

We, officers of Directorate S, Department 12, of the KGB First Chief Directorate, have assembled for a traditional annual meeting in the office of Colonel Shcherbakov, our leader. The head of the country's Illegal intelligence, General Drozdov, is present. He is in a pre-New Year-celebration carefree mood, and before summing up the annual achievements says, 'As you know, the decision to establish your top-secret "biological" department was made with a personal instruction from KGB Chairman Yuri Vladimirovich Andropov.* He

---

* Yuri Andropov, who had been Chairman of the KGB since 1967, was appointed General Secretary of the Communist Party of the Soviet Union in 1982, and as such became the leader of the Soviet Union.

ordered its formation in 1980. There were some important reasons for this. At the end of the 1970s, Illegals started informing us about activisation of secret experiments in the West. These involved the genetics of dangerous micro-organisms. The information accumulated by intelligence was forwarded to the Politburo, as it was of the highest importance and priority. But even there this information was not for all; only those chosen were let into the secret.'

After thinking about what to say next, Drozdov continued. 'We also started to get more and more live biological material. For example, strains of Ebola virus were brought from Africa; from India, strains of smallpox. Although biological warfare, based on smallpox, was being developed in Russia already in the 1940s, Indian smallpox strains proved to be more effective. The Soviet Army is equipped with an American strain of tularaemia. It does not exist anywhere in nature. We obtained this strain in the USA.'

Drozdov's recollection is interrupted by Colonel Shcherbakov: 'Do you remember, Yuri Ivanovich, the Marburg virus?'

Drozdov nods: 'In the mid-1960s German scientists at a biological research centre in Marburg had created a vaccine against the East African haemorrhagic fever virus. But a tragedy happened – several members who took part in the dangerous laboratory work were infected and died. These findings caught our attention. Corpses of the dead were exhumed. Our intelligence was able to secretly send examples of infected tissue from the exhumed bodies to Moscow. Experiments with this biological material continue.* At the end of the 1970s our sources in the West managed to penetrate into top-secret laboratories there. Leaders of the Service decided to establish a new department in Directorate S – your Department 12, to keep the work in one pair of hands. Everything in one pair of hands – obtaining secret information and biomaterials, their first assessment and delivery into our secret biological centres, recruitment of agents, controlling Illegals, and carrying out clandestine operations, including acts of biological terrorism and sabotage in target countries whenever, and wherever, it may be required. We are not playing at spillikins with you here!'

---

* The work, the aim of which was to perfect a combat virus of haemorrhagic fever, continued for nearly twenty years. In April 1988, Dr Ustinov, a microbiologist who was working on modernising a Marburg virus in a secret Soviet biological laboratory, died after an infection. From his tissue was extracted a mutated virus, which got a new name – U Marburg virus – and was accepted in 1990 for use as a weapon by the Soviet army.

The general had ended with a grouchier tone of voice, and before our eyes he transformed from a good-humoured, aged man into a severe, demanding and imperious boss. (Before becoming the head of Directorate S, Drozdov led the KGB residency in New York. He made his career by participating in the freeing of Soviet spy Rudolf Abel from prison in America in 1962.*) We officers gathered in Shcherbakov's office involuntarily straightened our backs and sat upright in our chairs.

For me, this is the first such meeting. I am the youngest officer of Department 12, enlisted into the Service on 20 December 1984.

On my first working day I received a writing-pad with clean cipher-telegram sheets, a copy-book stamped 'top secret' for my reports, and a folder with Andropov's signed memorandum about our department's establishment. While putting the folder into my hands, Shcherbakov attentively looked at me and, with pauses – as if thinking that would be the best way to make an impression on a subordinate – he said, 'Read this, and keep your mouth shut! The fact that we are in the spy business is only half the trouble. For spying, one is punished if caught red-handed, but not severely! Well, they would expel you from the country, and that's it! But our department is taking part in a doubly unlawful business! Don't forget that our country signed the Convention! Even so, we help in perfecting biological weapons and preparing for biological war. If this is found out – imagine what kind of a worldwide scandal would break out!'

While reading the document, I was astonished by the department's high level of secrecy, what Westerners called 'compartmentation'. Every officer of Directorate S knew what the other departments did. For example, Department 1 (also called the Special Reserve Unit) had responsibility for particularly important clandestine operations performed by highly experienced Illegals. Department 2's task was the documentation of Illegals. Deep-cover agents of Department 4 operated in the USA, Canada, and Latin American countries, and Illegals of Department 5 worked in West European countries. But as for us in Department 12, officially we 'assisted the government in carrying out the state agricultural and medical programmes by

---

* Colonel Rudolf Ivanovich Abel, a.k.a. William Fisher, was the son of an old Boleshevik. During World War II he participated in radio-deception games against the Germans. He controlled a Soviet atomic spy ring in the USA during the post-war period, until he was arrested in 1957.

obtaining from overseas new fertilisers, modern medicines and biological products for medical, pharmacological and microbiological industries of the country'. But in fact we were supposed to obtain from the West the intelligence information which would help to produce and perfect Soviet (later Russian) biological weapons in many possible varieties. The list of the espionage targets (or 'main objectives', to use the language of the memorandum) included Western government departments and state commissions, intelligence services, ministries of defence, agriculture, health, environment, civil defence and emergency, secret military medical and biological laboratories – in fact anything connected with research in the field of genetic engineering and the most dangerous human and animal pathogens. The department gathered intelligence information about plans for and means of protection against the potential application of biological weapons in target countries.

Apart from that, we were also interested in which academic and, at first glance, unthreatening conventional research experiments with recombinant molecules and biological toxins could be applied to create new types of biological and toxic weapons. Our department was also interested in which laboratories, institutes, centres and private biotechnological companies were secretly involved in programmes to protect against bacteriological and toxin weapons. We had to investigate any possible security weaknesses associated with those organisations, and penetrate them.

The other task of our department was to obtain new strains of modified pathogenic agents, samples of other novel biological materials from the West's secret military medical laboratories, and secretly deliver them to Russian clandestine laboratories which developed and perfected their own offensive biological weapons. In Ken Alibek's book *Biohazard* there is no indication of any bioweapons research centres that were under the control of Directorate S's Department 12. It is possible he did not mention them because he simply did not know they existed. Biopreparat, where he worked, did not include top-secret laboratories that were under the control of the Soviet or Russian Foreign Intelligence Service; those operated as a secret within a secret, and were set aside for the creation of biological and toxin weapons for our clandestine operations in the West.

People were another of Department 12's prime interests: professionals in biological and medical fields, especially those who were involved in

34

experiments with recombinant molecules, toxins, and pathogens of dangerous human and animal diseases, which could be used for the development of a new generation of biological and toxin weapons. We were also interested in government and army personnel, and officials of intelligence services who had direct or indirect access to 'enemy' biological weapons programmes, as well as those who provided security for biological weapons laboratories and centres. Our goal was to recruit some of these people as special agents. We also recruited foreigners who could be used by the department as auxiliary agents. For example, those who could help to document and support the cover stories of our Illegals, or even help in liaising with them.

In the memorandum one continually met the phrases 'The Instance', 'Day X', and 'direct actions'. By 'The Instance' was meant the Politburo of the Central Committee of the Communist Party of the Soviet Union. After the disintegration of the Soviet Union, 'The Instance' came to mean the 'President of Russia and his Presidential Council'. The formula 'Day X' meant the beginning of a large-scale war against the West. 'Direct actions' implied acts of biological sabotage and terrorism against the civilians, the army, and the economy of a potential enemy. 'The potential strike targets' meant civil targets, including public drinking-water supplies, food stores, and processing plants; water purification systems; vaccine, drug and toxin repositories; and pharmaceutical and biotechnological plants. The other targets were classified as military biological and medical research laboratories; biological warfare munitions stockpiles; military garrisons and bases; and military biological defence commands, including those that were looking after surveillance of biological weapons activities. The list of all potential targets could be extended. Genuine information about targeted objects was also vital for us so that if an order came from 'The Instance' (say, the coming of 'Day X') we would be ready to use our people in the West to carry out 'special operations' – acts of biological terrorism and sabotage – against the 'enemy's' territory. These actions were to be implemented using the weapons of biological warfare developed in our secret laboratories. Our 'tools' for these actions included Illegals whom we had planted in the target countries and also the most reliable, well-trusted special agents. Stepping ahead of myself, I should add that in 1992 Department 12 was united with Department 8, which was responsible for planning and carrying out acts of terrorism and sabotage and launching diversionary missions in target countries in the event of war. And the task of executing 'direct actions' gained essential sharpness.

Although this must remain a matter of conjecture, I think it is quite possible that at the end of the 1980s the Soviet Politburo's plans included, as an option for a final resolution of the problem of the world power balance, one decisive strike using biological weapons created in secret biological laboratories controlled by the KGB and the GRU (Soviet and Russian military intelligence). At the end of the 1980s, the Soviet Union began the mass production of highly effective biological weapons, stored extra supplies of them, and prepared the means of delivery, including cruise missiles. At the time, the Soviet Union was the only country in the world that could start and win a global biological war, something we had already established that the West was not ready for. What an enormous and cumbersome organisation it was – Biopreparat, Bioprom, Glavmikrobioprom, secret biological laboratories under KGB and GRU control, factories and plants, and even secret military towns! And, last but not least, the Intelligence Service.

While reading the memorandum, I was surprised to see that there were no 'junior operative' positions in our staff grading system. Graduates of the KGB Red Banner Intelligence Institute started their service in Department 12 directly as operational officers, i.e. one rank higher than was the usual practice in Directorate S. Later, we jokingly compared our department with the Russian space-vehicle launch site Baikonur – extremely fast, like a rocket, launching the career of the next department head. Thus, Colonel Yuri Shcherbakov and Colonel Igor Patrikeev were promoted to deputy chiefs of the head of Directorate S, and Colonel Leonid Andreev (a protégé of KGB Chairman Vladimir Kryuchkov), who led us for one year, was promoted to the top executive level in KGB Headquarters. Before becoming the General Secretary of the Communist Party of the Soviet Union, KGB Chairman Yuri Andropov was a member of Department 12's Communist Party organisation. Officers of our department had unrestricted access to other directorates of the centre: offices of the SVR's chiefs were the only places to which we were denied access.

During my early days with the department I managed to become acquainted with nearly all the team. I quickly noted that there were two generations present: young people with special biological and medical tertiary education; and experienced officers, or 'veterans', who were not trained in any of the sciences. And before the meeting another person had approached me.

'Let me introduce myself. I am Colonel Valery Butuzov. Here, in the department, you will see me rarely – mostly on pay days. Just joking! I appear here whenever our top brass gets wrapped up in something serious and need some biological muck for operations. Officially I am a senior research scientist in a pharmacological institute creating new medicines. But, in reality, poisons and toxins are secretly made there, as well as psychotropic drugs. I also consult with the leadership at Biopreparat. Or the people there ask us for some "new medicine" from the West. Well, you'll know everything soon enough!'

Butuzov was an 'undercover'. Our undercovers were not supposed to appear in the department without special permission, and their work with operational files had to be carried out at secret apartments. They had to maintain the image of ordinary, normal research scientists; to publish articles in scientific and popular journals; to participate in scientific conferences; to take part in research projects and carry out their duties in government health commissions. Their names were not even listed in Directorate S's top-secret internal telephone directory.

As well as Butuzov, there was another undercover – Lieutenant Colonel Vladimir B—n, a doctor of biological sciences, who officially worked in the Institute of Virology of the Russian Academy of Sciences. He was one of the scientific advisers of the Academician Baev, the late head of the Russian Academy of Sciences' counterpart to the Human Genome Project. Vladimir B—n secretly supervised that area of research in the interest of our department because specialists had predicted that the results of the international project could also be used for military purposes – for the creation of a new generation of biological weapons.

Every young officer of the department would become a 'scientific under-cover' before being assigned to a 'target' country to perform clandestine work. It was assumed that such non-traditional cover would enable us to control the Illegals and agents more securely without arousing suspicion in local counter-intelligence services. When I was enlisted in Department 12 there were only two undercovers, but the number increased later on. I myself became an undercover in 1990, when I began to prepare for secret work in England.

Butuzov and B—n acted as intermediaries between Department 12 and secret biological research laboratories. They personally passed along to them samples of new micro-organisms, vaccines, antibiotics, serums, drugs, toxins and other biological materials gained by our agents abroad. They also prepared analytical reports for the heads of the Intelligence Service, who needed 'clever biological' recommendations on especially important operational cases. But neither Butuzov nor B—n ran Illegals and agents. That work was carried out by our aces – the true professionals in the secret war.

See how many of them have gathered for this pre-New Year meeting! Colonel Leonid Leonidovich Bouz had recently come from the KGB residency in New York, where he worked under cover as a correspondent of the Soviet media agency TASS. He was to direct the 'American' Section of the department, and was fated to play a big part in my life. Sitting next to him was Colonel Aliev, Shcherbakov's deputy, who had recruited agents in the East – in Iran, Turkey and Afghanistan. The other veteran, the nice, good-natured Colonel Chepornov, had recently returned from Germany, where he controlled a husband-and-wife team of Illegals codenamed TREFY. And there sat a very composed Colonel Oleg Sergeevich Dolzhenko, who until quite recently had been wheeling and dealing in Sweden. His secret agents operated in Britain, Scandinavia, and the USA.

Apart from me, there were so far only two young officers in Department 12, Captain Dmitry Kashirin and Major Abubakir Sh—v. But they cannot be thought of as beginners any more. Dmitry has already received a Red Star medal for his operations in Afghanistan, and the Kazakh Abubakir, called Bek by close friends, was running a spy ring in the World Health Organisation. The three of us and the two undercovers had biological or medical degrees. The 'veterans' had broad experience of secret work in many countries and had, over the course of many years' work, developed a quick grasp and very specific spy reflexes. We could be certain that if they spotted some foreigner who could be valuable to the department they would do anything to win him over.

Our veterans' task was to pass onto the younger generation their practical intelligence experience, and to teach us how to work with people of different temperaments and cultural backgrounds. They had to help us to develop the qualities and skills – and teach us the unwritten rules of survival

– necessary if we were to thrive in the always jittery atmosphere of Directorate S. Without mastering the latter, a successful career would not be possible. The aim was to help us newcomers become real 'wolf-hounds' in intelligence work.

At the end of the meeting Colonel Shcherbakov introduced me to my new colleagues. 'Our new officer. He'll work in the European Line. For the start you will look after him, Colonel Dolzhenko. Teach Alexander all the spy tricks that you know. And from him you can also learn something new. Alexander, please state the theme of your PhD!'

Shcherbakov must have anticipated taking some pleasure from the effect he thought the theme of my PhD research would have on my new colleagues. I named it: 'Molecular dynamics of tetrapeptides and their conformational structures.' To an inexperienced lay person, it had to sound something like 'abracadabra'.

'Repeat, please!' Shcherbakov said.

I did. There was total silence. After a short pause my patron said with a smirk, 'Well, Alexander, what a clever chap! Thanks! Most enjoyable!'

But the colonel was curious to see if anyone in the room understood anything of what I'd said. He asked once again; silence, which Vladimir B—n broke first: 'Yuri Ivanovich, I understand what Alexander is saying, but can't explain it.'

And then B—n offered to play the same game with the theme of his PhD dissertation. Then General Drozdov himself roared with laughter. 'Stop tormenting us old dogs!'

Towards the end, he warned the veterans, 'Your subordinates are smarter than you! They are the "bright lights" and soon will take over your chairs!'

As he left, he joked, 'Never ever again will I set foot in your department; you are all way too clever! You'll make a fool out of me one day, even though I'm your boss!'

Of course, the general was kidding. Neither he, nor the KGB Intelligence Service's heads, ever let our department out of their sight: the subject of biological war was becoming a hot topic in the world.

Chapter 2

A Double Life

My double life began in 1982 the day before I graduated with a Master's degree from the Biological Faculty of Moscow State University (MSU). It should be said that the state authorities had never shifted their attention from our faculty. Their interest was intense. In the 1950s, when the Soviet Union was testing its atomic and hydrogen weapons, the Ministry of State Security was instrumental in establishing MSU's Biophysics Chair. By government order, the chair (which was directed by Professor Boris Nikolaevich Tarusov for its first twenty-five years) worked almost exclusively on the problems of biochemical protection of human beings from the effects of radiation. And then, when the Soviet Union had begun to create a new generation of biological weapons, Academician Yuri Ovchinnikov, Vice President of the Soviet Academy of Sciences and the scientific leader of the Biopreparat programme, established a new Bio-organic Chemistry Chair.

Sometimes Ovchinnikov gave us lectures. Students of this chair yearned to be his PhD candidates because this assured them a fast and successful scientific career. But some people thought him a little crazy: it seemed he was unable simply to work or sit still in a chair; he was always dashing off somewhere, surrounded by a team of secretaries. Invariably flustered, he would rush past people without stopping to converse. He hurried through life, and died very early.

Many students from the chairs of microbiology, virology, molecular biology and bio-organic chemistry underwent their graduate work in collaboration with secret biological laboratories, which were involved in the Biopreparat programme and were a part of Glavmikrobioprom, the chief agency for the microbiological industry. After earning their degrees, students from those academic disciplines were most frequently distributed to the secret laboratories. As our Biological Faculty was preparing future research scientists for the Academy of Sciences, it was also a nursery for research scientists for the country's military-biological complex. In addition we student-biologists earned further qualifications as military microbiologists and parasitologists.

Due to Academician Ovchinnikov's efforts, a scientific research centre was established in the town of Puschino-on-Oka, about one hundred kilometres south of Moscow. With more than ten research institutes and laboratories, the Biotechnology Centre was for us students a collegial extension of our own faculty. There I carried out research experiments for my PhD, which I presented at the Biophysics Chair in 1987. My research was carried out on physiologically significant biological molecules – neuropeptides, regulators of human memory and behaviour – and was connected with the creation of biological molecules with specific properties. My researches also had military applications. For example, they could be used for the creation of a new generation of biological weapons.

About 1981, right at the start of my fourth year, I started to notice people taking a strange interest in me. One of my lecturers asked unexpected questions about my attitude towards military service. Our course's tutor was almost bluntly curious. He asked if I would agree, after graduation, to work in a field closely related to the protection of the state's essential interests? And I was asked something quite similar by a leader of the course's student Communist Party group. By the end of my fifth-year studies I had started to suspect that my future career, rather than being academic, might turn in an entirely different direction. But exactly which way I could not foresee. I thought that it might be work in some super-secret research institute or biological centre.

Each year the academic council of the Biological Faculty of Moscow University selected five graduates for doctoral study. In 1982 I found myself among those who were selected. I was elated; for a provincial in the Soviet

Union, after two compulsory years in the Soviet Army and five hard years of study, to become a legal resident of Moscow and to start a successful academic career had to be seen as a fairy tale. Doors into the highest levels of science were open to me! But the same day that the academic council's decision was announced I was asked to visit the university's tall building to have a chat with 'a man from the tenth floor'. That was where the university's Communist Party committee had its offices.

Life offered me two alternative paths – one from the faculty's academic council and one from the 'man from the tenth floor', i.e. either a pure academic career as a scientist or a career as an intelligence officer. I chose the latter. Naturally, at the time I did not understand that it was an offer of a job in Directorate S, the inner core of the KGB's First Chief Directorate, the foreign intelligence service. But I thought that it would be interesting, dangerous, 'foreign work' on the other side of the Iron Curtain. I felt I could not but agree. Of course, at that stage I did not even know what exactly I was agreeing to. Nor, it could be said, did the people from the KGB know exactly what they had in mind for me. That would only become apparent to them, and to me, as I underwent training.

Later, when I became acquainted with the practice of selecting candidates for Directorate S, I realised that propositions such as the one offered to me on the 'Party's floor' were always preceded by a long period of secret study, surveillance and background checks. It was normally not less than two years before a candidate would be approached with an offer of a job. The checking was so thorough that it got as far as the candidate's second or third cousins living in Kamchatka or in the Aleutian Islands at the other end of the world. And even the hidden thoughts of the candidate could be be checked out. Unaware, the person was secretly surrounded by support agents and placed under surreptitious surveillance. To my surprise, I learned that nearly all the rooms of the student hostel in the university's tall building on the Vorobyov Hills – or, as we called it, 'GZ' (the initials of the Russian words for 'main building') – were equipped with permanent listening devices. Later, as my colleagues at Department 12 jokingly reminded me of the events from my student life, I realised that I had been meticulously watched and checked nearly from the beginning of my studies.

My fiancée was checked no less thoroughly. She was a student of the Journalism Faculty at Leningrad University, whom I had already known for more than two years. We had decided to get married as soon as I finished university. My new, covert friends allowed me to tell my future wife where I was going to work and what kind of life awaited us. Unknown to me, my covert bosses had clearly thought us an ideal pair, having found not one blemish in either of our lives, nor in those of our relatives.

My new superiors wanted me to continue my scientific career, to obtain my PhD, and to function in some way as one of their representatives in the Russian scientific community. I was supposed to lead a double life, as a scientist with a credible record in published research and as an intelligence officer.

At the end of spring 1982, I went through a medical examination in a KGB clinic in one of the small courtyards off Varsonofievsky Lane, close to Lubyanka Square, which was hidden far from strangers' eyes. In this clinic I successfully passed all the psychological tests designed to gauge my attentiveness. One of the psychologists was a graduate of my own faculty. She put me in a seat in a noisy corridor in the most unsuitable place, i.e. close to the flapping entrance door, and gave me a bulky folder with multicoloured pictures, figures, circles and triangles. All for a task on logic. She switched on a stopwatch and disappeared. 'Solve the task – and we will see what you are!' After I'd completed the puzzle, we sat in her office and recalled our Alma Mater and our favourite eccentric lecturers. Some months later, after graduation from the university, my wife and I left Moscow for Tarhankut peninsula in the Crimea to have a summer holiday at 'our place'. 'Our place' was where I used to spend my annual student vacations in a Biological Faculty research facility established for the purpose of studying dolphins' 'language'. It was where, in the summer of 1980, I had actually met my future wife.

I returned to Moscow not long before the qualifying exams for doctoral study. That was when I first met an officer from Directorate S – Lieutenant Colonel Eduard St—ov – who worked in the department for the selection and training of Illegals (Department 3). Later on, when we became friends and colleagues, Eduard revealed that in my first years at the university my future was put into the hands of two intelligence departments at once – Directorate T (Scientific and Technical) and Directorate S. Directorate S, more influential and powerful, seized me from its rival.

After meeting with Eduard St—ov, I was put at the disposal of Department 3 of Directorate S and became PETER – my first codename. I regularly met with two mentors: Eduard and Captain Alexander S—n, both of whom had also studied at Moscow State University. Their being graduates of my Alma Mater drew us together and created a family atmosphere; we shared a sort of 'aura of the dedicated', which can only be understood by Moscow State University's graduates in Russia. Two years passed under their guardianship.

Firstly, at the conspiracy apartments of Department 3 we had intense conversations, the conversations of like-minded confederates. Eduard and Alexander asked me repeatedly about my years in the army and at university. Then they produced numerous booklets with psychological tests and I had to answer enormous numbers of questions. I wrote essays on given or freely chosen themes. Soon I was introduced to the practical basics of my future profession. The main goal was to teach me how to come easily and quickly into close rapport with people we might wish to cultivate, 'objects of interest' or targets, to draw them out so as to obtain frank disclosures from them about themselves, and to establish their key data – full name, age, place of birth, working and home addresses, and their contacts. I was trained to cultivate such first contacts either as informal friendly relationships or as friendships. So, after first meetings, I had to try to use these contacts to obtain secret information. That was what establishing successful contacts was about, my new teachers pointed out. I had to make these contacts in an unobtrusive manner; and, most importantly, to explain to my contacts, without arousing their suspicion, why I wanted the information I was obtaining from them. And all of this was just a part of the early stages of managing a relationship with 'an objective of operational cultivation', while following the long-established procedures necessary to guarantee the secrecy of our 'operation'. In Russia these procedures are called *konspiratsiya*. Besides key data, what we called 'determined and personal data', I had to be able to fish out as much additional information as possible from my targets.

At that time I was asked by my superiors to undertake a number of training tasks. For example, I had been given orders to 'penetrate' what were then prohibited, private viewings of kung fu movies from Hong Kong and pornography. Whether or not I was fond of these assignments, I could not refuse to carry them out. All these jobs were skilfully camouflaged as genuine 'military tasks'. I found out about their true training purpose – to test covertly my reactions to complex and difficult conditions – only two years later when I joined the intelligence service. To my surprise, from time to time in the corridors of Directorate S I came face to face with some of my former targets, who I then saw were intelligence officers who'd played the roles of 'agents', 'dissidents' or 'specialists'.

In 1986 I had one year of training at the Andropov Red Banner Intelligence Institute of the KGB, the forge of the Soviet Union's professional spies.

Not much is written about the Andropov Red Banner Institute. We called it simply 'KI' after the initial letters of the words 'Red' and 'Institute' in Russian. It is mentioned in a few memoirs of former officers of the Russian Foreign Intelligence Service. Some have outspokenly ridiculed the Alma Mater of Russian spies, and described clichéd routines and flourishing formalism. Others remembered their training in KI as a period of great enthusiasm and hard study which helped them to become true spy masters.

I studied at the KI's one-year faculty. It was located in the north of Moscow, on Flotskaya Street, near the Rechnoy metro station, and occupied all of an unremarkable school-style building.* A sign on a doorway announced that it was the 'Computing Centre for All-Union Scientific Research on Industrial Information'. Just try to figure out what hides behind that! Close to the metro station, about two kilometres from the faculty, was our training 'villa'. It was fenced off from the outside world, a three-storey training complex with classrooms, rooms for psychological training, a gymnasium, cafés and a student hostel.

---

* It is interesting to note that in 1992 the Japanese Aum Shinrikyo sect opened its Moscow branch on Flotskaya Street. The sect even received permission to broadcast prime-time programmes on a central Moscow TV channel to promote its ideas and beliefs about 'supreme intellect'. The leader of the sect – 'His Reverence' Asahara – often appeared on these programmes. In March 1995 the sect became known worldwide following its Tokyo subway attack using a deadly nerve agent, sarin. A year earlier the sect had sent an expedition to Zaire (now the Democratic Republic of the Congo) to seek and obtain strains of a deadly Ebola virus.

I wonder who it was in Moscow that gave shelter to this strange sect? Who benefited from it? What was hidden behind the veil of the sect's widely publicised 'supreme intellect'? And why did the FSK permit the sect to open its office on quiet Flotskaya Street of all places, where many KGB–FSK offices were secretly located?

Among us KI students, there were those who had already served in Afghanistan, Syria, Iran and Iraq as military advisers, or as officers of the intelligence branches at various levels of Soviet troop command. Some were even decorated with military medals in recognition of service in these countries. All of us were under thirty years old, and full of enthusiasm.

Training in the KI involved finding places on Moscow streets suitable for clandestine momentary (a.k.a. 'brush') contacts and dead-drop operations; interrogation of 'work-ins' (volunteers); cultivation of 'objectives of potential recruitment'; making 'recruitments'; work with 'spotters' and 'agents'; detecting external surveillance; microdot preparation; copying of 'secret' materials; studying secret writing; sending and receiving radio and code signals; psychological training; learning how to deceive lie-detectors; and studying foreign languages. It is impossible to name all the skill sets and competencies required in a successful would-be spy. Living in the 'villa' was meant to be an imitation of the work of the intelligence officer in a 'legal' KGB *rezidentura*, i.e. operating from a Soviet embassy, consulate, etc., in a target country using legitimate Soviet documentation and generally with diplomatic immunity. Training at the 'villa' was continuous during our year of study. The last exercises occurred just before graduation when, during a two-week period, our skills and ability to undertake recruitment and intelligence work overseas were thoroughly tested.

My favourite part of KI were lectures and seminars on operational set-ups in the target countries and about their secret services. It was interesting to listen to stories of experienced officers who still seemed to reek of the smell of powder from their well-remembered and recent 'unseen battles'. Best of all were the seminars of Colonel Lebedev, during which he talked about his work in Britain, a thorough study of which country was part of my personal operational training. Colonel Valery Krepkogorski, who worked in the USA under the cover of one of the United Nations' commissions, stuck in my memory because of his great intelligence. He considered Mossad to be the most effective intelligence service in the world. There were also some eccentrics about. A retired colonel who lectured about the Chinese secret service had gone Chinese after his long years working there – a Buddha-like smile never left his face under any circumstances. The faculty's head, grey-haired Colonel Victor Tsuryupa, walked majestically along our building's corridors surrounded by an aura of respect. It was not surprising; he was a grandson of one of Lenin's comrades-in-arms, a man who was buried in the Kremlin wall close to the leader of the world proletariat and whose name embellished one of Moscow's streets!

And much can be said about various retired elderly officers who played the roles of agents in our student games. It was said that one was always keen to have a tipple of booze at a meeting, and that 'if you don't have a mug handy, do not try to make a "recruitment pitch" to him'. Another would not converse unless he had a crib sheet slipped into his palm by a cadet. With a third, any rendezvous had to be arranged not far from a public toilet, so he could dart in and out every five minutes.

My group's teacher-in-charge, Colonel Yuri Efimov, did not like me from the outset. He did not like the fact that, on principle, I did not swear. He did not like my independence – I never visited his office to blow the whistle on my teammates, as many other cadets were spooked into doing by our 'usher', i.e. our form-master. He tried to break me, and others. And he succeeded, the bastard, with many students in our group by threatening to give them negative references if they did not demonstrate their personal devotion to him. First one, then another of my colleagues slipped into the office of our usher to 'have a heart-to-heart talk'. By mid-term nearly half of our group was in Efimov's clutches. Somebody repaired his Volga car. Seeking to gratify the boss, somebody else invited him home to 'meet the family'. And someone went hunting for rare medicines for him.

'Mug', as I nicknamed Efimov (on account of his glossy, puffy red face with treble chin, the product of a long-term indulgence in spirits), liked 'simple, open people', and in me he was confronted by a know-it-all who was writing a PhD. He could not understand how it was possible to write a dissertation while also undergoing a difficult training-year in KI. What a smarty-pants that Alec is! I didn't like my situation, but the fact was that I could not see any way out of it. My chiefs in Directorate S insisted that I complete my dissertation as soon as possible so that I could retain my cover as a scientist. Colonel Efimov did not care at all. Quite the contrary; he did everything in his power to prevent successful preparation for my orals, which were going to be held almost a week before the start of the last training session at the 'villa'.

My life in those days was indeed hell. Remembering it now, I cannot believe that I endured it. After classes I got to my flat at the other side of the city, in south-west Moscow, when it was already dark. My time was allotted literally by the minute. I had to write my dissertation at night in order to meet the deadline. I usually had five hours sleep a night, six hours if I was lucky.

In contrast with my classmates, I very seldom used Sundays, our one day off, to scout around for sites suitable for future meetings with 'agents'; cultivating 'foreigners', 'agents of influence' or 'trusted sources'; searching out dead drops, sites for posting conventional graphical signals (such as an 'X' on a pole, signalling a meeting); or preparing routes and potential places for detecting external surveillance. My Sundays were usually spent going to meet my thesis supervisor, and spending time with him and with those whose task it would be to critique the dissertation; or working at my typewriter to complete the thesis, and prepare a synopsis, tables, figures, photos, etc. My wife helped me a lot. She managed to visit the printing-house where the abstract of my PhD thesis was to be printed. And she visited the university faculty to track down the numerous official records, references, etc., which were necessary for my thesis's official presentation. At lectures and in classes in KI, I deliberately took a seat in the most uncomfortable positions in order not to fall sleep. I could only get two days off from Efimov to make my oral presentation – and then only after a call from my 'patron' Colonel Shcherbakov, who had become a deputy chief of General Drozdov by that time.

My oral presentation passed successfully. The next day I was seated again at the desk in KI and my neighbour whispered to me that bets were being made in the group about whether I could defend the dissertation or not.

Efimov tried to label me 'unprofessional' and record in my personal files that I was 'not suitable for operational work'. Several times during training operations in the city, he tried to organise my capture. He even prepared a secret video camera to record my being caught red-handed at a dead-drop operation. Look, future generations of cadets, he would like to say, at how you should not operate! But I did not appear on the video at all – there were only confused and lathered officers who'd been the external surveillance; I'd identified their snares in time and professionally avoided them. Even now I remember Efimov's sour face when he had to name me as one of the best graduates at the end of the course.

They tried to 'break' all those in KI who even slightly stood out from the general pack. Everything that defied the usual stone-grey regime irritated our old-boy mentors. An initiative or a personal opinion was not encouraged in the Service. Maybe that is why there were not many really talented and extraordinary officers. For that special reason exceptions to the rule always stood out – those intelligent, talented and bright officers who were truly expert at their job. I am very glad that I had the opportunity to work with some of them.

I look on Colonel Yuri Shcherbakov, who was the first chief of Department 12, as my godfather in the Intelligence Service. An extraordinary man with initiative, he was soon promoted to deputy-chief of Directorate S. He, like most professional officers who worked with agents, had first astonished me with his ability to quickly win somebody's favour, instill in that person a level of trust, and thus gain influence over him. In reality, behind the welcoming surface, goodwill and 'warm reception' there lurked a human soul-catcher, that had been chiselled out and refined over many years of professional work.

I sincerely regretted Colonel Shcherbakov's leaving Department 12 – it was so interesting to work under his command. In Shcherbakov's period Department 12 functioned without unnecessary stress and rush. Unlike some of his successors, he paid serious attention to the selection of new officers to the department. He did not hurry to employ just anyone on offer. Believing that it was not by the number of bums on seats that the quality of the department's work and its results should be assessed, he thoroughly vetted and trained candidates. He could not stand routine work-product from our overseas operations, and encouraged us to search out new approaches. He even joked, 'Give our department new, non-typical overseas posts which are not known to our enemy, and we will penetrate here, there and everywhere to keep the world in fear!'

He was keen to use and create covers and posts for us in foreign organisations. That would allow for more secret and secure operations with Illegals and special agents. The new posts would be separate from the KGB's legal *rezidenturas*, which operated out of our embassies, consulates and the like, and because of that attracted the constant attention of our enemies.

And Shcherbakov was very experienced. As a security officer at the Soviet consulate in New York, it was he who sounded the alarm when he suspected betrayal by Soviet diplomat Arkady Shevchenko, who was serving as United Nations Under-Secretary General and adviser to the Soviet Foreign Minister. He did that not long before Shevchenko's defection to the West in April 1978. And he would have managed to escort Shevchenko back to Moscow if the bumbling KGB bureaucracy had not given Shevchenko time to escape.

I met Shcherbakov in late autumn 1984 at one of the department's conspiracy apartments, in a narrow lane between Gorky Street and Mayakovskaya Square. The first person I saw when I entered the brightly lit room was a tall grey-haired man, about fifty years old. He energetically got up to walk towards me and introduced himself: 'Colonel Yuri Ivanovich Shcherbakov, the head of Directorate S's Department 12 of the KGB's First Chief Directorate.'

It was evident that he was the big chief. With his easy and unconstrained manner, he differed from the others at the meeting. Among those already well known to me, my mentors, Captain Alexander S—n and Colonel Oleg Dolzhenko, there were two more people.

'Our personnel officers,' Scherbakov explained.

Our meeting lasted about one hour. My new chief wanted to be certain what sort of a person he was admitting to his team. Stuttering slightly at the beginning of each phrase, Shcherbakov asked me to talk about myself. And then, unexpectedly, he asked me to speak in German. He had read my personal file and was purposefully trying to check whether I could speak the language. At the end of the meeting he summarised my nearly two years of assessment and training by officers of Department 3. He indicated that I would work in intelligence with Directorate S's Illegals, where I would use my knowledge of molecular biology. He did not supply many details: 'You will work in the centre and overseas. And you will run our agents and Illegals. We will talk about it later, in the department.'

Finally, he asked my military rank. As I mentioned earlier, graduates of the Biological Faculty, in addition to their main education, received military training. I answered, 'Lieutenant.'

'Well, let's start from Lieutenant!'

He cast a glance back to someone on his team and then back at me: 'Enlist Alexander in the department!'

Chapter 3

My Colleagues

At the beginning of 1984, the KGB's First Chief Directorate moved from the old building on Lubyanka Square into a new complex located in the south-east Moscow suburb of Yasenevo, just over the Moscow Ring Road. The sign on the main entrance said: 'Scientific Centre of Strategic Studies'. Who would be fooled by that? Certainly not the CIA.

The officers nicknamed the place 'the Forest'. And the complex of buildings behind the barbed wire really was surrounded by forest. Directorate S used seven floors of the twenty-two-storey building – from the fourteenth to the twentieth floors, sharing that space with the Scientific and Technical Intelligence (Directorate T) and External Counter-Intelligence (Directorate K). Our Personnel Department was also there. A place for Directorate S's Operational Technical Department was found on the twentieth floor. In addition there were two cafés for officers, on the first and thirteenth floors, the general cafeteria on the third floor, a conference hall on the twentieth floor, and under the roof was a furnace for destroying documents.

At nine o'clock in the morning, the Service's buses arrived from all parts of Moscow at the two main checkpoints. Together with the officers came teachers of foreign languages, department secretaries, and those who provided ancillary services – chefs, gardeners, shop salesmen, cleaners, boilermen, drivers, etc. At first, no more than thirty buses stood at the front of the main entrance each morning. By the end of the 1980s the car park had to be enlarged. The grove of trees behind the ferro-concrete fence was cut down, the trunks uprooted and the area asphalted in front of the second entrance. Now, over one hundred buses came into the Forest. The centre was growing into a large bureaucratic organisation. A new medical clinic was built. The car park for personal vehicles was also enlarged, and in front of the main entrance a shop was built to sell overseas goods. The shop was a most popular place for secretaries during lunchtimes. A duck pond was built between the central buildings of the centre, along with an indoor swimming pool with see-through glass walls, sports halls, and open tennis courts. A shooting-gallery was built on one of the underground floors. There were facilities for learning foreign languages, cafés, a cinema, saunas. There were book-stalls selling titles not available to ordinary Muscovites. There were internal checkpoints with armed guards, and of course there was a marble Lenin on a pedestal. I wonder if that Lenin is still looking after the life of the Forest?

Department 12 received nearly half of the nineteenth floor for its use, sharing it with Department 8, which at the time was led by the severe Brigadier Vladimir Alexandrovich Kostikov. We were assigned more than fifteen offices in contrast to the few we'd occupied in the old building in Lubyanka Square. Our veterans used to joke that 'Thank God, at least here we won't see the back of Iron Felix turned away from his Chekists'. (The statue of the founder and first boss of the Bolshevik Cheka – the forerunner of the KGB and its Soviet predecessors – was on Lubyanka Square, and faced away from the KGB's main building.) Some of our rooms were empty, awaiting newcomers.

In the department there were three main sections, called 'lines'. Each section was responsible for operations in a particular geographical region of the planet. They were the 'American', the 'Asian', and the 'Western European' sections. By the end of the 1980s, the last had extended its area of activity to the former French colonies in Africa.

Each of the three geographical sections had to establish and constantly replenish its lists of main and second-priority targets, including academic and civil objectives – first of all in the NATO countries. We determined the second-priority targets rather quickly. For example, within two to three months my Western European Section prepared operational memorandums about these objectives. Only in three major countries of Western Europe –

Britain, West Germany and France – were there any significant concentrations of targets, around one hundred in all.

USA and Canada were the main targets of the First ('American') Section. Latin and Central American countries operated as supplementary beachheads for work directed at their northern neighbour. Into our department in 1987 came Major Mikhail M., who, 'with the smell of gunpowder' still about him, arrived from Mexico after his successful work in the local KGB *rezidentura*. He came back, as we used to say, 'with results'. He was put in charge of the American Section in place of Colonel Leonid Leonidovich Bouz, who was sent by General Drozdov to lead Illegal Intelligence at Directorate S's station in East Berlin.

I first heard of Mikhail M. in 1985 when I had laboriously to reconstruct a secretly taped conversation between him – a Line N Illegal Support officer in the Mexico *rezidentura* – and an Illegal, who arrived for the rendezvous from the USA. The meeting took place on a busy street in town. The city noise was a nuisance as it was hard for me to make out the details of the conversation. I had to wind and rewind the tape back and forth, until, finally, it was possible to piece together a clear picture of their talk.

Straight away I noted that the conversation was professionally structured and our officer had thoroughly prepared for it. At the start he inquired whether our Illegal had any difficulty while crossing the Mexican border and whether he noticed anything suspicious while his documents were checked, whether his baggage was checked by the customs officers, and how comfortably he had settled into the motel. Not wasting valuable time, he asked questions about the Illegal's settling into American society, about the safety of his cover, and about old and new contacts which our department asked him to pay close attention to. There were talks about the Illegal's recent visit to an American city, where he secretly picked up some documents from an agent through a dead drop. The agent was working in some research centre or a central government department, and the material was very important for us. The documents were quite valuable, so Mikhail asked for the details of how the operation was carried out. Mikhail did not interrupt much, and I understood that he was thoroughly involved in the Illegal's work in the USA, and that such a meeting was not his first. I realised that Mexico City was one of those where meetings with the Illegal were carried out, but that he actually operated in the USA, where he supported an agent who was very valuable to the department. Towards the end, Mikhail asked if the Illegal had any personal requests. There were none.

My report – a few typed pages with the deciphered conversation and a brief analysis of the main questions touched upon during the meeting – was put onto the desk of my chief, Colonel Oleg Dolzhenko.

'I listened to the tape before you,' he said. 'Notice how logically and concisely they talk – nothing irrelevant. Our officer saves time! The conversation is carried out on foot, but they also have to control the situation on the street. Learn!'

Oleg Dolzhenko was coaching me for independent work with our Illegals.

I asked Dolzhenko about the package that our officer had given to the Illegal at the very last moment.

'You noticed! Very good! It was money from us and letters from his wife. They haven't seen each other for three years.'

The career of Major M. was going along quite nicely. Situated in Mexico from 1982 to 1986, he took part in cultivating an American who, it was hoped, would be a valuable source of secret information. And he established a trusting relationship with the contact. Soon after Major M. returned to Moscow, that person was recruited and we started to receive highly important secret information from him. In 1989 Major M. was awarded the Order of the Red Banner. During the festive ceremony in our department, General Drozdov said, 'Congratulations Mikhail; you persevered in cultivating this man! But N.' – Drozdov pointed at one of the officers of the Latin-American Department, a veteran of the Service – 'you didn't really believe we'd be successful, did you? Didn't believe that we could win him over. You almost gave up on him. Well, a successful job gets an award: N. only gets a certificate of honour from the KGB Chairman, while Major M. receives a combat medal.'

The officer who finished the long recruitment also received the military order. Straight after the ceremony Mikhail M. received early promotion to the rank of Lieutenant Colonel.

It seems that this source of valuable secret intelligence information was recruited in 1987 or 1988. It usually takes one to two years for Directorate S to be sure of the new agent's genuine co-operation with the Intelligence Service, by rechecking the validity of the secret or operational information

56

using its own methods of verification. The Service celebrated recruitments, decorating its officers with combat orders only when highly valuable agents from the main enemy – the USA and NATO – were recruited. So, from 1987 or 1988 our department ran a deeply hidden and thoroughly protected agent in the USA who had access to quite serious secret information. Contacts with the agent were reduced to a minimum. Personal meetings with him – one, or at most two per year – were organised in different countries on the American continent, where an American – a carrier of serious secrets – could freely travel for a holiday without arousing suspicion. Usually, it would be Mexico or one of the countries of Central America, where Line N officers of Directorate S's local stations could meet with the agent. I do not exclude the possibility that the agent was a high-ranking official of the United States intelligence community or that the agent worked either in the US Defense Department or in some other government organisation dealing with biological weapons issues. When definite secret information was coming from him, an Illegal or even several Illegals could be used as go-betweens to make that person's contacts with Department 12 more secure.

At the very beginning of the 1990s, the American Section grew tremendously. To its four existing officers were added several graduates of KI who had postgraduate qualifications in biology and medicine. More often than the others, the American Section received new biological materials from its sources on the American continent.

From five to eight officers operated in the European Section during my years in the KGB and its successor. Each usually had three or more valuable and promising agents, Illegals, not to mention newly cultivated potential agents. Inclined towards very competently run operations, Colonel Oleg Dolzhenko, a real wizard, knew the methods and cover documentation process of Illegals, which he'd learned from his years of work in Department 2 – the one concerned with the documentation of Illegals. There, at the end of the 1960s, he had met Oleg Gordievsky and actually shared an office with him in KGB Headquarters on Lubyanka Square, before he left to work in the KGB *rezidentura* in Göteborg, Sweden. Because of his connections with that 'enemy of the people' Dolzhenko suffered after the sudden disappearance of Colonel Gordievsky at the end of the summer of 1985.

In the year of Colonel Gordievsky's defection to the West I was a junior officer and had been working in Directorate S less than a year. I was told by my bosses not to come to the Forest more than once or twice a week unless on special request. Not to stand out in the centre – that is what was demanded from me.

During one of my occasional appearances at the centre I was a witness to how a few officers of our department received a questionnaire sent out by the Investigation Commission that was sorting out the circumstances of Gordievsky's disappearance. Everyone who had met up with GNUS, or VILE, as Gordievsky was codenamed by the investigation, had to declare in detail where, when and under what circumstances they met up with the traitor, and who else was present and what they conversed about. All case files with which – to any degree – the defector had contact were taken apart in the most harshly minute and scrupulous detail. The Investigation Commission tried to sniff out all evidence of the circumstances of Gordievsky's escape, and track down all his contacts with officials of the centre.

The defection of Gordievsky, as well as the escape of Major Kuzichkin three yeas before in Iran, damaged the careers of those officers of Directorate S who had worked with them, or who had dealt with cases and operational files which were run by the 'turncoats'. Our 'elders' – Colonels Aliev, Chepornov, Bandura, Dolzhenko and Leonid Bouz – became objects of suspicion. That resulted in long 'digging' by the Investigation Committee into their personal files, which considerably annoyed them. But even such thorough investigation by the commission did not prevent some of the same officers being sent, some years later, on overseas tours of duty, to Bonn, Vienna and East Berlin.

Of course, only bad things were said about Gordievsky after his escape. All his sins were remembered, and his actions were pulled to pieces. Veterans of the Service who knew him personally remembered that, for example, when a student of KI, Gordievsky kept his distance from his classmates. They said that the 'arrogant' fellow always abstained from invitations for a glass of wine in a bar after training in town. (Of course, since then the Russian mass media have written about him as an inveterate drunkard.) The drinking was a tradition between KI cadets and their external training-surveillance instructors during cadets' 'booting' on Moscow streets. But

Gordievsky's 'unfriendly' behaviour in the 'harmonious' Chekist group was seen as 'alienation from the team'. It was also remembered that his brother was an Illegal and also worked in Directorate S. The family stigma was also pinned on the brother!

It became customary not to talk about Gordievsky, not to be interested in his past or to ask unnecessary questions of those who once knew him. His name remained only in files he had worked with. In 1991 I began preparation for my overseas assignment to England and started to study materials about the operational situation there. The first thing that I noticed when I opened the file was the full signature of Oleg Gordievsky outlined in a thick black frame, as if a funeral notice in a newspaper. Clearly, it was the work of some amateur fan of black humour.

In the footsteps of Gordievsky a few other intelligence officers of the centre defected during the next two to three years. They offered their services to the CIA and MI6. All of them held junior positions in Political Intelligence, where Colonel Gordievsky also had worked. Close friends – experienced senior officers of my department – shared a secret with me. They assured me that, for the most part, those escapes were active measures of the centre to mislead the Americans and the British. After the CIA arrested Aldrich Ames, one of its own senior officers, for passing secrets to Russian Foreign Intelligence, the revelation of Gordievsky's betrayal was laid at his feet. Presumably, Ames knew that MI6 had a very important mole, a source of secret information in the Forest, and he reported some of the mole's identifying details to us, from which the identity of Gordievsky was deduced. Whether correct or disinformation designed to shift the attention of the CIA away from another possibility – namely that, besides Ames, there was in place in the CIA or in MI6 headquarters another, possibly deeply, hidden source of the Russian Intelligence Service – is hard to say. However, that might not have stopped the other side from speculating.

My boss, Colonel Oleg Dolzhenko, did well at placing new Illegals in the West and working with them. He knew and used every possible type of communication with his sources overseas. Forever loaded with work, he swam through it like a fish travelling downstream, especially during interesting operations. I always tried to learn from him the art of secret spy work overseas, to learn even a small facet of what he knew and was able to do.

All his operational files, which I became accustomed to, I read page by page, fully absorbed, as though they were the most interesting detective stories: communication with Illegals in various countries, their annual reports and cipher telegrams to the centre, our clandestine checks on them.

Dolzhenko had always worked with first-class material – Illegals and prominent special agents who were foreigners – and never with agents placed in the West via the legal immigration channel. He did not consider the latter to be a serious source of secret information. He was especially energetic when operating preliminary training assignments, or as we called it the 'run-in' of Illegals in Western countries, especially in those situations where knowledge of the minutest details of 'black' work was required. He was an uncomfortable man for careerists to deal with because his character interfered with their pen-pushing. If there was a question of the safety of Illegals, he allowed himself to debate even with the Directorate's highest superiors.

I remember one extraordinary incident. My boss was awaiting a cipher telegram from the KGB station in one of the Scandinavian countries, about a successful border crossing by an Illegal codenamed ANVAR, who was on an assignment in Western Europe. Dolzhenko could not understand why, on the appointed date, a cipher telegram had not come to him. Without the message, the centre could not give permission to the London *rezidentura* to put cash and a new passport for ANVAR in a dead-letter box so he could continue his assignment. Did the KGB *rezidentura* miss a graphical code sign from the Illegal or did something happen along the route? Two days passed after the deadline before everything became clear. The telegram was mistakenly sent by the *rezidentura* to Drozdov, head of Directorate S, who sent it to one of his deputies. For some reason the deputy sent it to Department 3 rather than our Department 12, and only afterwards was it received by Dolzhenko, who ran the Illegal, and was supposed to have received it first. My boss called down thunder and lightning: 'The telegram made a round in the hands of the Directorate's heads! Just look at the comments on it! And my man is sitting somewhere in London without money and documents!'

Then Dolzhenko received an urgent call from Drozdov: 'Where is our response to London? Why are you taking so long with the answer?'

Dolzhenko swore at the big guns: 'I hadn't slept for two nights; I didn't know what to think. I had to remind Drozdov about just who was supposed to receive the high-priority telegram first. Now it is too late to break a lance over; the situation has to be fixed immediately. We will have to hand over papers for ANVAR through the emergency channel.'

Later, when ANVAR finished his assignment and returned to Moscow, there was an investigation of the accident.

During the year I spent under Dolzhenko's tutelage, I was able to learn a lot. I was very lucky that before I started independent work in Department 12 I had undergone the coaching of so professional an officer, a person with a distinct and contradictory character.

Two entirely different people lived simultaneously inside him. The first, serious, restrained, balanced, a profound professional of the Intelligence Service. The second, a person without humour, who was unable to compromise, unable to be patient or flexible.

Once Dolzhenko really surprised me. Together with a young woman who was an Illegal, we were driving in an operational car, windows blocked by curtains, to one of the conspiracy apartments. We talked about Russian culture. The aristocratic and lovely woman with polite and gentle manners, who had just returned to Moscow for a short break, was upset about how Russia's spiritual heritage – its Orthodox churches – were crumbling. Why were they not properly looked after in the homeland: 'In foreign lands, Oleg Sergeevich, you can acutely feel the separation; home is so far away! One feels the distance from the motherland quite sharply. Just how far is the road back? Especially when you see a preserved functioning Russian church. They look after Russian churches in the West as if those temples were their own heritage. It's so amazing!'

'Why amazing? Who needs these old ruins? Might as well demolish them,' Dolzhenko said.

'Are you serious, Oleg Sergeevich? I don't believe you! How can you, a Russian, not appreciate them? Will you treat me the same way once you don't need me any more?'

At times Dolzhenko reminded me of the fanatic Bolsheviks of the 1917 Revolution.

Dolzhenko was proud of his other Illegal, who operated in England, but one day he suddenly started to complain about him.

'I arrived in Sheremetevo airport, and there he was; sitting in a restaurant in the frontier border zone, slowly eating his dinner with a knife and fork like some prim Englishman. An hour passed, but he didn't seem to be in a hurry; he ordered coffee along with liquor! He started smoking a pipe. He sat back in an armchair and didn't notice anybody, as if he were in his homeland – England! Well, what a rascal, I thought! In the car, when we had already departed from the airport, I let it all out. I smacked him on the shoulder, as a signal for him to stop the masquerade, he was back on home soil. But he didn't leave his role, that strange chap!'

I remember that, during our first meeting, Dolzhenko disconcerted me with a sudden alarming question: would I be able, if the KGB requested so, to dispose of someone who was inconvenient for the Service? He said: 'Would you be able to kill?' And then, more specifically, he said, 'Kill him?'

The question was asked in Dolzhenko's everyday manner, sharply, abruptly, like an unexpected blow to the forehead; it had no connection with our previous conversation, and he asked it with fixed, unblinking eyes. Evidently, he was counting on catching me unawares so he could examine my reaction. Or, perhaps, to catch my confusion and surprise.

I enquired what arms I would be given to eliminate the person and who would give the order. It seemed to me that the direct question at first did not reach the tough colonel, that he probably did not expect it, but then I saw that he was pleased. 'Excellent reaction, well done!'

After that, Dolzhenko did not try any psychological tricks in our meetings.

He smoked a lot, so his eyes were always bloated from cigarette smoke. When my wife first saw him, she said, 'What a scary looking man! He reminds me of a ragged, exhausted wolf!'

As the years passed, that similarity grew greater.

He was from that clan of officers who felt most secure in extreme situations, who worked with all their might to the limit of their strength. That rhythm of work was his natural element. Living through the lives of his Illegals, isolated by the tall fence of the centre from the outside world and all of its complexities, he was helpless in everyday situations. His wife gave up on him; they divorced. 'Commercialisation' of the Russian Foreign Intelligence Service, the new trends of the 1990s, he did not, of course, accept. He resigned in 1993. Maybe, now, he attends the meetings of the

Communists or has become a member of the Russian Liberation Movement? Neither would surprise me.

The creative tension that Dolzhenko brought to operational work was not sustained by everyone. Some were jealous of his success. One such was another officer of our section, Colonel Evgeny Antonovich Bandura, who was quite narrow-minded, and certainly was not equipped for complicated operations. 'In our department, they think that only Dolzhenko works and the rest of us are just fools!' Bandura groaned. He may have been close to the truth.

Once, Bandura was put in charge of running one of the department's sources in West Germany, an agent who had successfully penetrated an 'objective' and gained access to confidential documents on new biological materials. Without providing skilfull guidance, Evgeny Bandura had the agent flood the department with mountains of secondary information, putting the diplomatic bag to regular use. At least once a month, Bandura received hundreds of pages, which, without analysing them himself, and without sorting them, he passed to Directorate T for evaluation. He did not care that Scientific and Technical Intelligence often found them to be 'materials [of] reference interest [only]' or, in better cases, 'for internal use only'. Bandura was simply not up to being involved in delicate professional work with a valuable agent. He could have wrecked everything by overworking the agent and foolishly exposing him to discovery. Oleg Dolzhenko's heart ached when he saw a heavy packet being carried into Bandura's office. Once he said, 'What a nutcase! Why do we need this pulp literature? Are we some sort of Salvation Army service? He'll ruin the valuable agent! For him the agent is like a saddle for a cow!'

Behind his back Bandura was talked about very openly in the department. They said he'd bashed his brains out through his feet while he was a Kremlin cadet, marching around 'Post Number One', guarding Lenin's body in the mausoleum in Red Square. Neither an expensive, high-quality cloth double-breasted suit, nor imported boots, nor 'professorial' horn-rimmed spectacles, could make Bandura seem intelligent and of noble appearance. No matter how hard he tried to play the role of skilled and experienced professional, his loud-mouthed nature was bound to come through. With a sharp, suspicious glance, enormous conceit, confidence in his own infallibility, and his way of ignoring the statements of anyone lower in rank than himself and interrupting them to say, 'I know just what nonsense you're saying!' he was seen as a person who loved only himself. To our relief Bandura cadged an overseas assignment to the Bonn *rezidentura* in 1989. After three years of 'feats of arms' in Germany he came back and was forced to retire.

A former officer of Department 5 (special operations in Western Europe), Major Leonid Petrovich Duganov, began work in Department 12 in 1988 – straight after returning from a tour of duty in Belgium.

The transfer of an officer from one operational department to another was uncommon in Directorate S. It was especially uncommon in the case of Leonid, who had no biological or medical degree. Even the fact that Duganov had worked in Department 5 with Major Gennady Varenik, who'd been arrested and executed for espionage on behalf of the Americans, did not interfere with Duganov's transfer to our top-secret department. There could only be one reason for this: during his tour of duty in the KGB's Brussels *rezidentura*, Duganov had sniffed out a source – evidently highly valuable and important for our 'biological' department. To facilitate exploitation of this source, without revealing the main operational and intelligence tasks of our department, Drozdov had to order the transfer of the valuable source to our department along with the officer who'd recruited that source. The case is analogous to that of Major Mikhail M. from the American Section.

In 1987–8 Department 12 trapped another valuable source in Western Europe. Someone in a quite high position who had access to secret information within NATO Headquarters.

Department 12's head ordered our secretaries to type up all Leonid's documents as a first priority. His ciphers were sent to *rezidenturas* in Western Europe marked 'urgent'. In that period, Duganov, as well as his superior Dolzhenko, provided his people overseas with only UK pounds as foreign currency, nothing else. To me, that fact reinforces the conclusion that the source was from Britain. I remember that Dolzhenko discussed the possibility of using one of our Illegals in the Scandinavian countries to assist Leonid's agent.

I remember another officer of our European Section, Colonel Alexander Mikhailovich Chepornov, as a kind and open person. He was keen to give me practical advice. Not long before his assignment to Bonn, Chepornov visited me in the Intelligence Institute. He said, 'Alexander, borrow more books and learning materials from the operational library. Take heaps! You don't really have to read them – no time, maybe, but do borrow them! They look at how a cadet performs in his KI studies – and here your are, with everything in place even here!'

I took his advice. Not long before my PhD submission he gave me more: 'Let's check all your opponents and who is in the academic council! We will use our central agent registration data. If someone is an agent, we will "work" with him and instruct him how to deal with your presentation!'

I laughed and refused. 'Even if one of them is a KGB agent, the quality of my thesis won't change!'

Chepornov specialised in the German-language speaking countries first of all, Austria and West Germany. When, at the end of the 1980s, he was sent to the Bonn *rezidentura* as a security officer of the Russian embassy, he dismissed the matter with a joke: 'I'll build bridges between the KGB and the BND; we have *perestroika* anyhow...'

Once I got into a conversation with him, when he found out before the submission of my PhD thesis that I continued to visit Puschino. It turned out that the biotechnology research centre located near Moscow was well known to him from when he'd trained to be an Illegal.

'In my time, it was just a small village,' he said, 'most likely even a settlement. I was sent there to check on how I could settle into a new, unfamiliar place. My legend? A demobilised soldier. Cover documents? If you don't count the worn-out soldier's papers forged by the Service, I had none. And my clothes were appropriate: soldier's blouse, boots, breeches and a suitcase. It was summertime...'

He told me how he reached the place, how he came out to the only field in the village. But where was he to go next, what was he to do? Anyone else would have been lost. But he thought to himself: 'Where is it easy to meet someone and establish necessary contacts? Maybe in a workers' dining-hall? No; that is populated only during lunchtime. During other hours it's empty – so, all contacts are in the public eye. That means it's not suitable. The day is ending – where to spend the night? Hotels didn't yet exist in the town. I went down to the river bank. Two merry women were tanning on the sand. I sat down nearby. We started a chit-chat. It turned out that they were a superintendent and a matron from the new student hostel. They said, if you help us drag mats into the gymnasium, we'll get you in! I dragged the mats, then spent the first few nights on them. There's more. I lived in the hostel. With my forged soldier's book I got a passport from a local police station. Girls helped with my registration, and I even found work – only thing I needed was to register at a new working place. For two months I lived in the village. I selected dead drops for contacts with my controllers. I completed all the tasks assigned to me!'

In the spring of 1991, a year of active intellectual ferment and intended changes in Directorate S, Colonel Chepornov moved to a new directorate which was responsible for co-ordination of joint work with the newly created secret services of the Newly Independent States. In autumn of the same year, he was shot dead by a sniper in the mountains of Tajikistan during an official trip to the former Soviet republic. This incident was widely reported by the Russian TV news programme *Vremya* (*Time*). Chepornov's coffin was placed in the old KGB Headquarters building on Lubyanka Square so that his colleagues could pay their respects. I remember him with gratitude and warmth.

In our European Section Colonel Arkady B., Doctor of Technical Sciences, held a special status. He came into our department from Directorate T. Before his promotion and transfer he operated for a long time in Vienna under cover of the International Atomic Energy Agency (IAEA). He ran some valuable agents in that organisation and served as an additional link between us and the Scientific and Technical Intelligence Directorate, where we regularly sent secret documents obtained in the West.

The Asian Section was for a long time small, just a chief and three officers. The focus of its attention were the countries of South-East Asia, the Pacific rim, and the Near and Middle East. Colonel Akyl Rakhimberdinov – a Russianised Kazakh and a fanatic skier – was its permanent chief. In spite of being over fifty years of age, he skied better than any youngster in all our competitions. Hardened by vodka, his iron constitution was more capable than those of his much younger skiing competitors!

Another officer of that 'line', Major Abubakir Sh—v, who in addition to English knew Chinese, siphoned off all the routine work of the section. He gobbled up lists of World Health Organisation (WHO) employees. If we were looking for candidates for cultivation, we just had to ask him to help.

But our approaches were not always successful. Once we became interested in a Chinese man who worked in Geneva, directing a section devoted to the surveillance and control of epidemiological diseases. The Chinese had access to information which was important for us, on communicable diseases and epidemiological outbreaks caused by deadly viruses around the world, as well as about developments of vaccines against these diseases. We found out that while he studied in Moscow in the late 1950s he had a Russian girlfriend, about whom he still had the warmest memories. In China he held an outstanding post in the Ministry of Health. And, judging by the information of our Service, he most likely worked for GRI (the Chinese Intelligence Service). With the help of a KGB agent, a high-ranking public health official in the World Health Organisation's Geneva headquarters, we organised a visit for 'our' Chinese to the Crimea and the Caucasus on his way back to China. We surrounded him with our people and used cameras and recorders wherever it was possible so he could be listened to and photographed. We found his former girlfriend and organised an 'accidental' meeting with her in Moscow. We hoped his recollections of Moscow, the university, his youth, and his first love, would mellow him out. And, once having 'relaxed', he would become more vulnerable, would want new meetings, and would venture into informal contact with us. No matter how hard Abubakir tried, nothing worked. The woman did not help, neither did the fact that they restarted their friendship, which resulted in correspondence between her and the Chinese. Nor did any of our other operational measures achieve any success. He was a tough nut! And we spent a year trying to 'reach' him in China and in Geneva, using our *rezidenturas* and agents in both countries. We did not manage to find a key to him…

From Abubakir I took two cases dealing with specialists in the WHO Headquarters. The first one, a 'trusted' spotter codenamed BELANOV, was a research-microbiologist ('trusted' in our operational jargon meant a person not yet recruited by the Russian secret services, but who had agreed to help and provided confidential information). The second one, a KGB agent, was a deputy minister of the Ministry of Health in one of the Soviet Baltic republics who supervised a whole section in the Geneva Headquarters. From both came information about WHO officials – specialists we were interested in – and confidential information from around the world, especially about development of vaccines against the most dangerous human and animal viral diseases.

During the period of disturbances in Kazakhstan at the end of the 1980s, Major Sh—v was urgently sent to Alma-Ata on Drozdov's orders. Under cover as an 'emissary from the foreign emigration centre', he had to penetrate the main centre of the anti-government organisation which had provoked the massacres, the marches and the disturbances. For several months, he lived and operated in the republic on an illegal basis, using a forged passport issued in the name of a foreign citizen. And quite successfully, for which he was recognised by KGB Chairman Viktor Chebrikov.

In 1992 Abubakir Sh—v was given cover as a member of the official representation of the Republic of Kazakhstan (one of the Newly Independent States) in Moscow. Now Abubakir is an international relations manager in one of the biggest Russian gas companies. Perhaps that was his next operational cover?

Our department head's deputy, Colonel Ismail Murtaza-ogly Aliev, was an oriental joke-teller and admirer of pilaf and seasoned Scotch. He spoke several Farsi (Persian) dialects, knew some other Middle Eastern languages and understood the Middle East perfectly. He controlled the most important agents and Illegals who operated in the Asian Section's target countries.

Colonel Aliev was born in a small settlement in Iran which, in the late 1920s, became part of Soviet Azerbaijan. He received an excellent tertiary education in the humanities, graduating from the Eastern Languages Faculty of Baku University, and was preparing for an academic career as a philologist. He was greatly interested in ancient manuscripts and Iranian history. In Directorate S everybody knew and respected the talented and experienced Aliev. For long years he operated from *rezidenturas* in Iran, Pakistan and Afghanistan. To his credit he had recruited several valuable agents and had established trusting relationships with influential central government officials of the countries in which he'd been stationed. He was closely associated with Nadzhibula, the former President of Afghanistan, who according to Aliev was an agent of the Soviet Foreign Intelligence Service. Aliev had been awarded several combat orders and medals for successful recruitment of highly valuable agents and long years of fruitful work with Illegals in the 'tough' Near and Middle East region.

After the sudden disappearance of his former subordinate Major Vladimir Kuzichkin in 1982 from the Tehran station, Aliev was not allowed to be posted to KGB *rezidenturas* in the West. Either Aliev knew too much or it was a form of punishment for not having spotted the traitor in his department. Many times Aliev asked Drozdov to post him at least to East Germany, which was the only 'overseas' shelter available to many of Directorate S's exposed officers. But Drozdov persistently refused. It seems he reasoned that the secrets of Illegal Intelligence had to be kept close by his side.

'I don't understand anything about your microbes or your test tubes!' Aliev said. 'But I really know how to operate in the East, or with Arabs in Europe! It is a very particular category of people! Today he is your close friend, and tomorrow you won't notice how he will deceive you. To cultivate and work with that kind you need special talent and good personal relations!'

But compared with Dolzhenko, who hated Gordievsky for sabotaging his career, Aliev never mentioned anything bad or derogatory about Kuzichkin, notwithstanding the fact that Kuzichkin had defected to the British. When one of Aliev's friends brought him Kuzichkin's book *Inside the KGB*, published in England in 1990, he remarked after reading it, 'It's pleasant that he remembers me with kindness. Usually, those who flee scorn their ex-colleagues, especially their former bosses!'

An excellent storyteller, with carefully veiled Eastern humour, possessing the rare quality of not forcing his opinion onto his subordinates, Aliev was the centre of attention in all our tea-parties and table-talks. 'To drink tea' was a regular event for which we assembled, to celebrate the awarding of a new rank, awards, overseas assignments or somebody's birthday. Gorbachev's 'dry law' was in force throughout KGB Headquarters. At the end of some working days, the department secretaries Lyudmila and Tatyana would set up a table in the far corner of the nineteenth-floor corridor – far from the bosses' eyes.

During that time, when my wife and I did not yet have our own apartment in Moscow, we often had to move from one rented apartment to another. On one of these 'tea-drinking' occasions I was given an electric frying pan for my thirtieth birthday. 'So you can cook your dinner while you move,' Aliev said.

He told us that in Iran, where there was always a big problem in finding clean water, they had to drink whiskey, 'So the microbes could be killed. Because Iranian enteric bacillus was everywhere. The best antidote I found was ripe Scotch. Whatever the microbe, the whiskey would deal with it! And I, of course, then washed it down with some rather bad Armenian brandy from the embassy shop. I would never wash it down with my best Azerbaijanian cognac!'

Aliev worked in the Service for more than thirty years and retired in 1992. Once he said, 'I, and maybe also Colonel Mikhail D—n, are the eldest in the Directorate. Whatever KGB *rezidenturas* he was in, he was always roaming in the local markets, looking for old coins [everyone in Directorate S knew Mikhail D—n's passion for coin collecting]. I, on the other hand, wandered about in graveyards, wondering how I could bring to life some cover stories for our Illegals.'

And yet, after all that, notwithstanding the friendly relations between officers in the department, no one really trusted each other. I believe that is the fruit of every secret intelligence service.

Instilled into us was a permanent internal assessment of one's own behaviour and speech, a fear to say more than was needed, or to 'open oneself' to a friend; or, even worse, to blow your cover by putting too much trust in the person who is talking to you. Such considerations dominated the behaviour and speech of the officers who worked for the Intelligence Service. The next distinctive feature is looking out for signs of increased and unusual interest in you by your colleagues. This is like having a machine in the brain which analyses others' words and actions in an attempt to find in them any faint signs of increased interest in your business. The habit becomes second nature and remains with you for years, if not for ever, and soon starts to influence your behaviour and style of speech.

In our circle asking too many questions about others was unacceptable. Immediately an internal alarm turned on. Excessive curiosity could cost you your career. In the best case an inquisitive officer might get a warning from the head of the department; in the worst, a call to Directorate S's Personnel Department followed by a threat to note in his personnel file that he 'cannot keep his tongue behind the teeth', i.e. he is too curious. Such a note in a personnel file was equivalent to a sentence of official death, the end of a career in the Intelligence Service. You could straight away discount the possibility of any tour of duty to the West and await the coming exile into a technical department or, worse, into the Research Institute for Intelligence (NIIRP), a so-called cesspool for failures and faulty officers.

Only one time, did Abubakir Sh—v try to snoop around in the office of his chief because he was interested in the documents on the boss's desk. Abubakir then had to explain in detail to the head of Department 12 why he was snooping. His own chief rumbled him! The department's head told us about this case at one of our weekly operational meetings as a means of warning everyone about the inevitable penalty for 'morbid curiosity'. I can imagine what might have awaited poor Abubakir if he had served us in Stalin's time. Morbid curiousity would have made made dead meat of him.

Captain Andrei F—ov, with whom I shared an office and whom I respected for his bright mind, innate tact, and excellent education, one day confessed that every time he found himself outside the centre's gate he felt uncomfortable among ordinary citizens: 'Seems like an escape from a prison to the free world! And to think that there is also a normal life without nerves, without constant stress. These ordinary people are so carefree and light-hearted!'

I felt the same, so used to an atmosphere of suspicion and anxiety that even during visits to the city on public transport I continued to analyse myself as if from outside my body, to maintain an inner reserve.

Chapter 4

VOLNA. My Working Day

Mail from the KGB's *rezidenturas* to Department 12 came in the name of GRADOV – the codename of the head of Directorate S – with an additional note, 'Line N-12'. The note meant that documents were for Department 12 only. We sent out routine correspondence to the KGB *rezidenturas* in the form of undeveloped microfilm in ordinary diplomatic bags and with the corresponding mark. For example, 'London, Comrade Petrov [codename of the London *rezident*], Line N-12' meant that the message was designated for the officer of Department 12 in the London *rezidentura*, or to the officer who handled Illegals on behalf of Department 12, if there was no Department 12 officer in the local KGB *rezidentura*.

Samples of biological materials and documents obtained by our special agents and Illegals were delivered to Moscow through two main channels. The first channel of delivery, the normal diplomatic bag, was used for sending secret documents to the department and, more seldom, samples of new drugs, pharmacological remedies, vaccines and other biological materials which could be preserved for a long time under normal conditions.

The second channel was an urgent secret-delivery channel codenamed VOLNA (wave). This meant delivering the material via an international flight of the Soviet Aeroflot airline in the pilots' cabin, where one of the pilots was a KGB officer. This channel was always used in urgent situations when active biological materials were being sent by our people – for example, serums, virus vaccines, diagnostics, novel micro-organisms, strains of potentially dangerous pathogens, biotoxins, etc. The VOLNA shipment was preceded by a cipher telegram from the KGB *rezidentura* to our department with instructions specifying the flight that would be used. At whatever time this telegram came to the centre, the Directorate S duty officer had to inform one of us immediately about the parcel that was coming; VOLNA could not stand delay!

I remember well my first trip to retrieve a VOLNA package. An urgent telegram came at the end of the work day. My boss Dolzhenko signed it upon receipt, and rudely remarked, 'I have a meeting in an hour with a departing Illegal! Drozdov is planning a farewell evening at a *kukushka*.* Can't miss it! So, you have to go get the VOLNA!'

The cipher telegram which preceded the delivery said: 'Centre, for GRADOV, Line N-12, for VASILIEV [codename for the head of Department 12]. Materials from ROSA sent by VOLNA. Airplane flight number X from Paris in X hours. MAKAROV [codename of the KGB's Paris *rezident*]'.

I requested a car. The dusk had already turned into late night when we came out of the Forest on a winding road. Coming onto a motorway, the driver put his foot on the gas. Even though we quite clearly went over the speed limit police officers did not stop us: our dark windows and the car's number plate clearly identified its passengers as belonging to the Soviet Union's highest authority. In an hour I was already in Sheremetevo. At the time the airport's KGB duty-room was found on the ground floor of the left wing of a huge building. I had to wait there for quite a while because the guard had not yet registered all of the mail arriving from the KGB's overseas *rezidenturas*. Around me, photographs of those who were being searched for by the KGB on a national level were hanging on the walls. I recognised Gordievsky's photo.

Soon, the usual formalities were finished: I'd shown my ID as an officer of the central KGB apparatus to the duty officer and signed the special registration. I hurried to the car.

The parcel was just a package of rigid white-foam plastic the size of a shoe-box. It was tightly sealed with tape. Light, weighing no more than

---

* KGB jargon for a conspiracy apartment or safe house.

a kilogram, it did not give the impression of being anything unusual. A modest package, it was similar to those which are often used by microbiologists to deliver bacterial and germ cultures. When I was a student, we used similar packages to transfer flasks from one laboratory to another. It was nothing unusual, at least for me. Yet all the same, the box could potentially cause death to many thousands of people.

We drove back to the centre at about 120 kilometres per hour. By then it was close to midnight. I hurried into the Directorate – to call the boss of the section to let him know that the materials had arrived safely – then placed the package into a fridge so that in the morning I could hand over the live materials, as requested.

At one point we'd had to stop at a red light while a passenger bus entered the road. In the lighted windows of the bus, I could see the faces of people who were sleeping, or reading the evening newspapers. Their work day had ended and they were hurrying to get home. They did not suspect that a deadly threat might lie in a small packet on the knees of the passenger in the government Volga behind them.

The work day had also ended for our agent in the West, and for the officer who had forwarded materials from him to Moscow Centre. They were probably relaxing. Everything had gone well for them; one had been able to extract biological materials, the other to receive them, without attracting the interest of the enemy's counter-espionage service. It was possible that a courier – an agent or an Illegal – had also been used to deliver the package from its source in a Western laboratory (possibly over more than one border), to the Illegal Support officer of the local KGB *rezidentura*.

I came home late that night. As usual my wife awaited my return. She had no idea where I had been and what I had done. But I was happy that my work day was finished and that things were going well.

I am certain that none of us – neither I myself, nor our people in the West, nor the Aeroflot pilot, nor the KGB officer who accompanied the pilot, nor the officers of the KGB post at Moscow's international airport who did not even know what kind of materials they were handling, none of us thought at the time that because of our actions the balance of war and peace might have swung towards war that day. To all of us, it was just another day in the midst of many, yet another delivery from overseas, yet another experiment in a secret army biolab...

Early in the morning, before the birds were awake, Colonel Butuzov rushed into my office. He asked me to hurry a delivery to the secret military biological laboratory in Kakhovka,* which itself was part of the secret military biological centre in Protvino.† I once had the chance to visit it. From Protvino to the actual location of the biological centre was twenty kilometres. The centre was hidden in a forest, cut off from the world by a high wall with rows of barbed wire and by armed guards. The entrance to each laboratory was guarded by people in civilian clothing, but they were KGB officers. The cafeteria for employees reminded me of army blocks. The laboratory windows looked like embrasures, and sets for liquefied nitrogen stood like lines of armed soldiers. The scent of agar-agar hung heavy in the air (agar is a growth medium and is used to preserve many micro-organisms). On the whole, the complex was a military city adhering to a rigid army-style of work. How many such secret military medical centres were dispersed across the broad expanse of Russia, in Obolensk and Chekhov, Podolsk and Kirov, Pokrov and Stepnogorsk, Sergiev Posad and Volgograd?

Afterwards, trips to pick up VOLNA materials became routine: once or twice a month, I received biological materials from England and from Germany. I surrendered each sample to Lieutenant-Colonel B—n or Colonel Butuzov, and with the department head's decision we passed it on to the secret biological laboratories and research institutes to be analysed for potential use in our biological weapons programme and in biowarfare modernisation. Relevant excerpts of the documents accompanying the VOLNA materials were sent to Directorate T, Scientific and Technical intelligence, after having been 'depersonalised' so as to avoid revealing details about their sources. From the classified laboratories and centres, as well as from Directorate T, we eventually received final evaluations of the documents and biomaterials obtained by our sources overseas. These evaluations were one of the criteria used in deciding the effectiveness of the department's work. Through our 'undercover officers' Butuzov and B—n, the secret laboratories and centres, in their turn, sent us requests to obtain secretly for them this or that novel strain of microbe, virus, live biological materials, or

---

* A Moscow city district.
† A town near Moscow.

the results of specific research experiments from the West, which would help them to perfect our biological arsenal. I remember only one or two occasions when a package with biological content in soldered test tubes, which had been received via the VOLNA channel during the night, was left in a fridge in the Directorate's duty-officer quarters. At the crack of dawn Captain Mikhail Sh—lov, the officer of the American Section who had delivered them from the airport the day before, took them to one of the secret biology labs which worked in liaison with Department 12.

Before the activisation of Department 12's work with overseas sources in 1987–8, biological materials often came to us without proper precautions having been taken for their containment. The containers in which they were delivered from the KGB *rezidenturas* were temporary and, frequently, not meant for the transportation of potentially dangerous biological pathogens. Sometimes there were no appropriate containers at all. In those days samples were forwarded almost always in the same packaging as they had been received from the sources. These might be soldered glass tubes, vacuum flasks, petri dishes, or thermoses with dry ice. The consequences could have been disastrous if dangerous micro-organisms had been accidentally released into the open environment. When poorly packaged materials were received, Colonel Ismail Aliev, our deputy chief, could be heard yelling, 'Guys! Don't drag any of that shit into the centre! The whole Intelligence Service will die! Carry all this stuff straight from the plane into the secret labs!'

And then he'd go on quite seriously, 'If the CIA find out what we are doing in here and how we bring this shit into the centre, then it will be a bad for us! They will slip in a double agent, and through him they can bring in anything they like! Straight from overseas and right into our pocket! That would be fun for "The Company"! The best way for them to wipe out the whole of our Service in one hit! Listen, can we leave all this to the CIA? Huh? Lets spread some germs for them on the road or somewhere else – perhaps inside their beloved CIA Headquarters in Langley?' Back then, this simply seemed to be 'black' humour.

At the time we laughed. But now I recall the sudden deaths in Department 12: Major Dmitry Kashirin in 1990 and Lieutenant Colonel Leonid Duganov in 1993. They were the most frequent receivers of VOLNA materials. Dmitry worked in the American Section. He had superb health, practiced karate, and loved to swim. He had been awarded the Red Star medal for missions in Afghanistan. Leonid Duganov, my good friend, worked in Oleg Dolzhenko's group. Just a few weeks before his death he called me at my home. He had a lot of plans for the future, was asking me about my new work. He said he wanted to see me and to warn me about something. Something was bothering Leonid about operational matters under Dolzhenko. But we weren't able to get together. Dmitry died very suddenly, in his house; Leonid in a KGB hospital, where he was rushed a week before his end. We were never informed what exactly happened to them. Asking questions was not acceptable. And I then thought the cause of their sudden deaths might be some dangerous micro-organism or virus or other biological material from accidentally unsealed containers that they had received via the VOLNA channel.

Now I think about what could have happened if an officer of Line N in a local KGB *rezidentura*, due to a blunder or misunderstanding, or because of some other circumstances, let out from under his control some potentially dangerous microbes and viruses. For example, if there was a threat that the agent or officer was about to be caught red-handed by local counter-intelligence while receiving biomaterial or on the way to the KGB *rezidentura* in a target country, what would he have done? Because, in most cases, the local, i.e. Western, counter-intelligence really could not know what operation was being carried out by the Russian Intelligence Service, they would not have known what containers had been handed over to the Russians. The consequences of an airplane crash on foreign territory or in our home country can scarcely be imagined. Likewise an automobile accident while potentially dangerous micro-organisms were being transported from a *rezidentura* to a Western international airport, or from Moscow's Sheremetevo international airport to Russian secret bio-laboratories. I suspect that the consequences of any such incident could have been catastrophic. And not only for one country, but for several countries simultaneously.

The danger of Western intelligence agencies using a 'biological Trojan horse' against the Forest was seriously discussed by Drozdov at one of the department's operational meetings. Soon an order was issued that all active biological materials received through VOLNA were to be sent immediately, following strict safety measures, to the secret laboratories and institutes that were working for our department on the biological weapons programme.

In order to secure the VOLNA channel in all the KGB *rezidenturas* from which Department 12 received biological material, we sent circulars explaining how, in the local conditions pertaining to each *rezidentura*, live materials had to be kept before forwarding them by the urgent channel. The first KGB *rezidenturas* to which we sent circulars were the two KGB stations in the USA, in New York and in Washington. Moreover, in order to work with our most active sources in the target countries from which biomaterials came regularly, we requested the Operational Technical Directorate (technical support) to prepare special-purpose containers for safe delivery of potentially dangerous pathogens to Moscow. These were then shipped out to the *rezidenturas*. The first section that did this was our American one. Its officers, more often than others, went to pick up VOLNA materials in Sheremetevo. Especially Captain Mikhail Sh—lov, who ran our sources in the USA, Mexico, Peru and Columbia. The activity of the American Section grew from 1987 onwards, when Major Mikhail M., who had been transferred to the department after his long tour of duty in the Mexico *rezidentura*, led it. As far as I can judge, starting from the end of the 1980s the American Section would have received up to twenty biological parcels from its sources on the American continent every year.

Even though my European Section was less active than the American Section when it came to obtaining live biological materials – usually no more than one or two VOLNA deliveries per month – their value was no less. Colonel Dolzhenko was most energetic in controlling our, at most, three or four Illegals who were actively working in Western Europe. During our annual meetings nearly all documents and materials stolen by Dolzhenko's people received the highest grade.

Despite its small size, our Asian Section, which operated in the countries of the Middle East, Central and South-East Asia, and the Pacific rim, also used the VOLNA channel – maybe not as often as the other two sections, but with considerable frequency. As far as I could judge by indirect signs, the most valuable sources for that section were located in Turkey, Iran, India, Singapore, Australia, and even in China. The Asian Section's irregular delivery of biological materials via VOLNA could have been explained by Aeroflot's less frequent flights within the section's countries; the difficulty of working in Muslim or Buddhist countries; and by the fact that our Illegals who had access to biological materials in those countries were not able to operate in close proximity to KGB *rezidenturas*.

And as for China, the reader should not be surprised that it was mentioned among the countries singled out for heightened attention by Directorate S. Russian Illegal Intelligence never let Communist China escape its attention – not least because China is the most powerful close neighbour of Russia, one which it has aided but also fears. Leaders of the Soviet Union were always interested in whether China would turn to walk the path of 'true Marxism'. Even after the Soviet Union fell apart and Russia became a country in its own right, there was still the worry about who China would side with if Russia happened to become involved in a large military conflict. Another vital issue for the departments is that China is one of the few countries whose citizens have dispersed over nearly the entire planet, and Chinese local communities are present in nearly every developed country of the world. That is why Illegals who have been documented as ethnic Chinese could readily operate not only in South Asia but also in the countries of the main enemy, including the USA and NATO countries.

The delivery of VOLNA materials was only a drop in the wide sea of my responsibilities. Mornings usually started with a read-through of telegrams from KGB residencies in Western Europe and, sometimes, from the USA. Most of the time these were notifications from Department 12's officers on the subject of operations carried out: the filling of a dead-letter drop, or a personal meeting with an Illegal or an agent. Afterwards, I received detailed accounts of those operations by diplomatic post.

By 10 a.m. I was already drafting rough replies for telegrams so that I could discuss them with the boss of the European Section, Colonel Yuri Zhitnyakov. If, on that particular day, he gathered all of his subordinates for a routine meeting, then I would have an opportunity to pinpoint for him the details of current work and could offer my ideas for follow-ups with the agents and Illegals.

The day did not always run according to plan: sometimes an undercover officer would suddenly turn up with another request from the secret laboratories. Then, we had to sit down to plan an assignment for an agent or an Illegal who would solve the proposed task. Or, at times, someone from among my colleagues, who had no specific medical or biological education, would unexpectedly request me to help him prepare an assignment for one of his sources in a target country.

Once a week, in the morning, there were operational meetings with the chief of Department 12. During these, we were allowed to ask for or to offer new ideas, but not to argue. Whoever misunderstood that found himself unofficially labelled as a trouble-maker. Sometimes the head of Directorate S was present at those meetings. Secret military biological research centres and laboratories gave their reviews and opinions about 'biological products' and intelligence information which was obtained by our people in the West. These reviews were discussed during the meeting. Our boss celebrated achievements and remarked on the failures of each section of the department, informed us about future overseas assignments, and encouraged and rewarded those whose operations in target countries were running successfully. Naturally, all of this was done without any mention of specific names, pseudonyms, city names, dates and even countries. That was a basic principle of the department's work – one was never to give out unnecessary information about one's own work even to colleagues. That kind of information was top secret.

One of my duties was to deal with Directorate S's Department 3. I regularly visited Department 3 for discussions with an officer who was in charge of the development of an Illegal for our European Line. I had to find out if the candidate needed any help when Department 3 surreptitiously made him or her undergo numerous tests for quick wit, bravery, perseverance, psychological equilibrium, etc. If he or she passed this 'exam' then it would be possible for the candidate to work overseas in more severe and dangerous environments. If not, then it was necessary to withdraw the candidate from training because we could not entrust our secrets to such a person. I could also ask Department 3 for a personal file that covered the candidate's training so that in my office I could more closely examine the reports of external surveillance, agents, psychologists and foreign-language teachers who were selected for the candidate Illegal. I could check to see if there was anything in those reports which would make us ponder whether the candidate would be a reliable colleague or not.

Sometimes people from Department 3 needed my biological skills. For example (just one of many examples I could give), Lieutenant Colonel Oleg Petrovich B., a former Illegal who had operated for more then ten years overseas, acquainted me with an operational file on an objective of interest to Directorate S. The papers showed that a middle-aged American woman, a research-biologist specialising in animal infectious viral diseases, had been put under observation by us. Results of her researches were being regularly published in Western mainstream scientific literature, but did not appear to be anything other than conventional academic research. Approximately one or two years before the described events, the number of publications of this woman had noticeably decreased, and very soon stopped altogether. For an active research scientist this was somewhat unusual, even strange. But it was not that which attracted so much attention from Department 12. It was the fact that she had changed the main direction of her research of many years' standing! After having published her first article on the results of her experiments about especially dangerous infectious viral diseases of humans and animals found in the Far East and in the countries of the Pacific rim, she disappeared from the pages of mainstream Western scientific journals. From a short article published in a local Singapore news-paper, we subsequently found out that the scientist had left her laboratory in the USA and was working in one of Singapore's scientific research insti-tutes. We managed to trace her movements – she actively moved regionally and often changed her places of work – and was doing research at bio-logical laboratories in Indonesia, Hong Kong and Singapore. We thought that was strange. Was she hiding something? What was the motivation for her increased researches in applied epidemiology of infectious viral diseases of that area of the world? Maybe she had begun to work for the US Defense Department? Was it possible to approach her?

I was told to assess the information collected about this American research specialist and to provide an analysis. This was to help Oleg B. to formulate a task for an Illegal whom Department 3 was training for us. During his training assignment to the countries of South-East Asia (where the Illegal was to operate), he was to obtain further evidence about the American scientist, this 'objective of cultivation' as we referred to her. He had to penetrate her circle of contacts and try to find out if her researches were for the United States' military authorities.

At the same time, I got ready several analytical reports for my department in which I enumerated and analysed the characteristic features of the vari-ous secret research laboratories where experiments on the most dangerous biological pathogens of infectious human and animal diseases could be carried out. These were to help our Illegals to identify potential targets in addition to the ones already known to us. Some of these reports of the early 1990s were directed to our neighbour – to Department 8, the department of sabotage and diversion support.

A lot of attention was paid to the regular reports of the Illegals. Before these could be read, I had to ask our Operational Technical Department to decipher the cryptography which our Illegals used and, at the same time, to check if any attempts to read the letters had been made by the enemy's counter-intelligence. This usually took two or three days.

I met with some of the department's Illegals, in conspiracy apartments during their short trips to Moscow for vacation or further training. Some Illegals I never met in person, but I knew them perfectly well from their personal files. In these meetings I had an opportunity to focus their attention on specific research experiments. For example, at the end of the 1980s we were particularly curious about genome modification of the most dangerous viruses – for example, recombinant virus-vectors with built-in dengue fever virus' genomes, Ebola virus, *Bacillus anthracis* virus, influenza viruses and other potentially dangerous pathogens. We were also interested in obtaining information on secret experiments with recombinant virus-vectors, including smallpox vaccine virus and baculovirus with viruses of dangerous human fevers. I remember an Illegal being taksed with gaining information about secret research dealing with the international Human Genome Project. Our client – the Biopreparat agency – wanted to know which genes coded certain types of human diseases. And especially about genes which are responsible for specific characteristics related to sex, race and other essential anthropological features. The latter might be used to develop a novel type of weapon – 'genetic' or 'ethnic'. From the middle of the 1980s, we gained information about experiments in the area of design of physiologically important proteins and peptides, which Russian secret biolabs could use to create peptides with toxicity higher than botulinum toxins. At another time we sought information about investigations of the structure, properties and biochemical activities of various deadly toxins and human hormones, particularly peptides or, more precisely, neuropeptides (regulators of memory) which control human emotions and which could be used as biochemical weapons. This kind of a weapon is ideally suited for secret terrorist operations in enemy territory: its covert use would result in short-term or long-term corruption of human mental processes, and induce uncontrollable feelings of fear and panic, and could even lead to death. Other sources in England were ordered to obtain any information about experiments that dealt with recombinant DNA vaccines and viral gene modification (including the influenza viruses), with the aim of using it as a living vector for applying foreign genes. And, of course, to gain the live material, as such. We were interested in development of vaccines in military medical laboratories in the USA.

Apart from Illegals, I also ran two valuable agents, RIO and YAN, as well as a network of agents which we created in the Western European countries, including Greece and Germany. Naturally, each agent and Illegal was unique. Methods that worked with one of them were not suitable for another. In each case, I had to search for new communication variants which differed from the ones already used. That meant that again and again I sent requests into the KGB *rezidenturas*, demanding that they select a place for yet another dead drop, different counter-surveillance routes, more places for momentary secret contacts and personal meetings, and many similar things. A lot of time was spent working out cover stories for Illegals. Nothing was ever to be repeated – that was a strict rule of Directorate S.

About once a month I went to a furnace situated on the top floor, under the very roof of the twenty-two-floor building, where I burnt stacked drafts of secret documents, notes, reports, letters and telegrams sent to the KGB *rezidenturas*, notes for Department 12's chief, my sector chief, and similar things. Under strict instruction, someone from among Department 12's officers was a witness to the destruction, to see that all the documents on the 'destroy' list were actually destroyed. As history shows, notwithstanding our efforts, documents were copied, were carried out into the open, and were handed over to foreign intelligence services. But these were exceptional cases. Everyone who was caught was tried and executed. During my service in Directorate S, Major Gennady Varenik was caught red-handed.

Four times a week, including Saturday, I took foreign-language classes in a neighbouring building. And I had quite an incentive: for demonstrated competence in each European language, we received a bonus of 15 per cent of our pay (25 per cent for an oriental language). I should mention that all officers of Directorate S received an extra 10 per cent for 'special secrecy'; work for Illegal Intelligence meant inclusion in the highest secrets of the country and we were obliged to keep our mouths shut tight as in no other directorate of the Service. My PhD brought me a further 15 per cent pay increase. With the bonuses for foreign languages, the special-secrecy bonus, and the PhD bonus added in, my pay was quite massive by Soviet standards!

Once a week we went to the KGB shooting-arcade where I was responsible for the military-sports training of our officers. I tried to see that no one missed training without good reason. In the arms room we could order up pistols of many different types and brands. I remember a very small, toy-like Scorpion machine-pistol with a block-button on the top of the barrel housing – a favourite weapon of terrorists – which was used, for example, by the personal-security guards of former Czechoslovakian Communist leaders. In our arcade each person could select a weapon to suit his own taste. Of all the brands, I preferred an American short-barrelled Colt, and I learnt how to shoot from this particular type of gun.

Sometimes we watched videotapes in an operational video library. The tapes were documentaries about serious emerging diseases, training operations in special Western military medical units and government services, and many other topics concerning deadly epidemic diseases, deadly outbreaks and biological weapons attacks. We had an extensive choice of this kind of information, because the operational library in the centre was regularly stocked with fresh overseas newspapers, journals and programmes taped from local and central TV channels from countries all over the world. Materials for specific issues that interested operational departments were regularly obtained and were delivered to the centre in Yasenevo from overseas KGB stations. For example, together with officers of Department 8, we in Department 12 watched a film about the spread of HIV/AIDS in Western European countries. It was shown specifically at our request.

When General Drozdov signed the order for my overseas assignment to England in 1991, I began training in several departments: in Department 8 (support of international terrorism and sabotage), in Department 5 (special operations in Western Europe), and in Group R (group for analysis of intelligence information).

If there were no urgent meetings or assignments to fulfil, my working day finished at 5 p.m. By 4.30 p.m. all documents had to be cleared from the tables, placed in their boxes and put into safes. The safe and the cabinet's door were sealed. The key was left with the duty officer. Then the Service's buses took us officers of the Forest home.

In 1990 I was put 'under cover' and began to appear at the centre quite seldom. In April 1992 I went to my office for the last time.

Chapter 5

Our People in Target Countries

By glory and dishonour,
by evil report and good report;
as deceivers, and yet true;
as unknown, and yet known;
as dying, and behold, we live...
II CORINTHIANS 6.8–9

Nearly twenty years ago the profession of spy or agent seemed to me, a young intelligence officer, very romantic and mysterious. I had an unstoppable urge to be an Illegal. After several years in Department 12 I asked for deployment to the West with a long-term secret assignment under an assumed name and life-cover story, i.e. as an Illegal. Colonel Aliev replied by asking, 'What's your current age? Twenty-nine? That's a bit old, although we've had people start training here as Illegals at thirty. I have no doubt that you'd manage. Some two or three years will be spent on training, then the run-in and ... shoot for the moon! The family, of course has to remain here; you and your wife won't be ready in time to work as a team: it's hard to document you both at your current age.'

And my colleague Chepornov added, 'Don't you understood yet, the difficulty of their lives? You come back to Moscow after fifteen or twenty years of work and you have neither house nor home. The Service will help of course. A pension will be given you, or some job. In the West our Illegals live with constant stress. But after adopting the Western lifestyle, they find it hard to settle back into the reality of our life. Illegals are loners, strangers in a crowd. Think about it!'

Before coming to work at Directorate S, Chepornov and his wife went through the whole training programme for clandestine work overseas as a husband-and-wife team of Illegals. They were documented as Germans – citizens of a Western country, preserving their roots with motherland West Germany. They were not sent to the West; just before they were to leave, Chepornov's wife became seriously ill and their mission was cancelled. If one understands that both candidates were training and preparing to be placed in clandestine work as a married couple the reason for killing the assignment becomes easier to understand.

The names of the majority of Illegals, no matter how much they did for the home country, are buried in oblivion, and it is rare that the motherland gives them what they truly deserve. The people who assign them never fully trust them. Many Illegals are forced to live apart from their families for many years, sometimes with unfamiliar, but 'necessary', husbands and wives, as the centre commands. Some even end up living on foreign soil until they die. Then they are buried under false names. In Moscow there are special boarding schools for Illegals' children who are born in Russia. They are children who never come to know their parents in close relationships.

One husband-and-wife team successfully worked for more than ten years in the West, mainly in France, while carrying out the tasks of Department 12, before finally returning to Moscow. Their children were born and grew up in the host country. When their plane landed in the Moscow airport, the parents revealed to their children who they really were and their real Motherland. The ageing, grey-haired, retired Illegal couldn't continue without tears: 'Our children were about to cast us off, demanding to be sent back home.'

During the Soviet era, not even the surnames of officer- or agent-Illegals who had long since finished their work could be mentioned. Of course, their work could not be hinted at in open publications. Nothing could be done: it is the rule of conspiracy – a condition of intelligence work in all countries, especially so in the case of intelligence derived from the work of Illegals.

It is interesting for me to read memoirs of former spies from both sides of the former Iron Curtain, especially the pages dedicated to the 'Illegals Directorate', i.e. Directorate S. Regrettably, in most cases the deceptions and the methods of training Illegals are far from the reality – perhaps with the exception of those found in Nigel West's book *The Illegals*, published in England in 1990.

There are few books about Illegals. I know of only two publications, written from a first-person perspective, which can be trusted. They are *Inside the KGB* by Vladimir Kuzichkin, a former officer of Directorate S who switched sides in 1982, and General Drozdov's book *Memoirs of the Head of Illegal Intelligence*, published in Russia in 2000.

During my service in Department 12, I took part in running five Illegals: two husband-and-wife teams, ROSA and ROMAN, and TREFY; as well as ANVAR. In the 1980s and the early 1990s, four of them were the most active in the European Section of Department 12.

The Illegal codenamed ROSA worked in England from the end of the 1970s under cover as a research-microbiologist. From the moment Department 12 was created in 1980, ROSA was transferred to us and began to carry out only 'biological' assignments.

She worked in a scientific-research institute in a town near London. The institute was involved in experiments with potentially dangerous pathogens of lethal human and animal diseases, and we justly presumed that it was also involved in England's covert biological warfare programme. By the start of the 1980s, ROSA's position was quite secure – her deployment in the country and 'planting' within its scientific community had been successfully carried out. The Illegal agent codenamed ROMAN, a molecular biologist by training, was sent as her back-up. The procedure of his infiltration counted on one simple yet complicated process – his marriage to ROSA. It was simple, because this variant did not require further measures to document ROMAN or extra operations to back-up his legend (i.e. his notional biography). But it was a difficult option because we were not sure how well the relationship would develop between the two Illegals, who differed ethnically: she was a Russian Jew, he a Muslim. Surprisingly, their marriage proved to be successful, which does not always happen in the case of Illegal families created at the order of the centre.

Postgraduate study for a PhD in one of London's universities was added to the programme of ROMAN's successful infiltration and legalisation. At our recommendation, he selected as the topic of his PhD study an area of molecular biophysics which had potential military application.

His primary task at this stage was to help ROSA to gain intelligence information about secret microbiological research experiments, and the secret study and cultivation of research-biologists and government officials with good prospects in areas of interest to Department 12 so that we could consider them for possible recruitment. Apart from that, we suggested that ROMAN be used as a courier between our sources in England and the Moscow centre.

ROMAN was an active participant in a karate group in a local sports club where members were postgraduate students and prominent young specialists at biological research institutes. Because of the overall interest in martial arts among young people at the start of the 1980s, ROMAN had good opportunities to establish informal contacts with people of interest to us.

Copies of reports about the results of experiments in her laboratory came from ROSA regularly. She also sent 'live stuff': test tubes and ampoules with cultures of new strains of potentially dangerous pathogens; cultured media, which were used for the safe keeping of micro-organisms and as substances in which they could multiply; and soldered ampoules with new vaccines which ROSA's laboratory got for carrying out vital control tests on animals.

ROSA's active participation was of a high quality – she sent up to ten parcels annually to the centre. A courier, another agent, handed over live materials from ROSA to Line N Illegal Support officers of KGB residences in Western European countries, mostly in Scandinavia. To arrange meetings and covert contacts with ROSA, we took advantage of her rather regular trips to the Continent, most often to France and West Germany, for science seminars and workshops with other microbiologists.

But in 1984 ROMAN died, shortly after finishing his PhD while both Illegals were on holiday in Italy. ROMAN lost control of the wheel of his car on a steep hill and died as a result of the crash. ROSA suffered a few broken bones, and after medical treatment she returned to England to continue her work.

One of ROSA's achievements was that she helped Department 12 to establish a clear understanding of what kind of biological protection and measures against potential covert biological warfare attacks England had during the 1980s and at the beginning of the 1990s.

The husband-and-wife team codenamed TREFY were citizens of East Germany who agreed to co-operate with Soviet Intelligence. During the mid-1970s they underwent special operational and intelligence training and from the beginning of the 1980s actively continued their work in Western Europe. The centre decided that they should settle in West Germany. Their cover was a private medical practice, as a result of which they acquired wide contacts in West Germany.

One of their tasks was to gather information about secret military medical and biological laboratories in Western Europe, especially in Germany, and the investigations that were carried out in them. Their other task was to seek out people who were involved in secret medical or biological experiments or who had access to them, who could be approached for secret co-operation with Russian Illegal Intelligence. Of course, actual recruitments were carried out not by TREFY, but by officers of Directorate S's Special Reserve Unit, Department 1 (who had been Illegals in the past themselves), or by Line N officers of the KGB *rezidenturas* in Bonn and Vienna. TREFY were also to establish the locations of all NATO installations; their command personnel; their main and reserve command points; food, air and water supplies of the garrisons of army and air-force bases; air-force bases, and cruise-missile and rocket sites. They were to find out the most preferable and convenient ways for taking out the personnel of those military objectives through the use of biological toxins and deadly bacteria in the event of war or a large-scale military conflict with Russia.

In order not to attract attention to TREFY, all personal contacts with them were held to a minimum. We operated with them only by using impersonal contacts, through dead-letter drops and via radio communication. Colonel Chepornov, who directed operations with TREFY, had the special responsibility of organising dead drops for them. Often he found places for dead drops behind condom machines in nightclub toilets. I remember joking with him about that: 'Alexander Mikhailovich! You must know the nightclubs in Vienna and Bonn as well as your own hand! Give me a hint, which one is the best. I might need the information some day.'

'Alex, unfortunately I don't know all of them,' Chepornov said. 'The higher-ups in the *rezidenturas* are trying to stifle my curiosity. Even so, as you can see TREFY keep up their high-life, and regularly visit such places!'

Only once every couple of years were TREFY summoned to visit secretly East Berlin and Moscow for more training and a short vacation.

Thanks to TREFY we received regular reports about work in several military laboratories in West Germany, and also about private pharmacological companies where, under Bundeswehr orders, experiments were carried out with pathogenic recombinant micro-organisms; with new synthetic herbicides and plant hormones for crop- and food-source destruction; and new antibiotics and vaccines against deadly viruses and bacteria. I remember that TREFY were able to obtain research reports about experiments using peptides, hormones that regulate memory and which act as controllers of human emotion Department 12 paid great attention to such substances from the mid-1980s, when Soviet military biologists were interested in the possibility of using genetically modified hormones as biochemical weapons of a kind which could be deployed, initially, to terrorise and disrupt a population. The secret pharmacological institute near Kakhovka metro station was especially interested in such research. That was where Colonel Butuzov often handed over biomaterials received from TREFY and other 'overseas' sources.

When I was left the Service in 1992, TREFY were still as productive as they had always been. Their value for us was so great that Department 12's European Section leader became their case officer.

To what extent, and how successfully, both couples – ROSA and ROMAN and TREFY – operated under deep cover in the West, can be judged in part by the number of volumes of their operational and other files. Just one operational file on TREFY added up to more than ten volumes and it could hardly be fitted into a single large office safe! That does not include additional volumes of operational correspondence with them. Judging by my own work experience, I know that in order to fill only one volume of an operational file with documents takes a year and a half, at least. Such a file – by rule, no more than 300 pages – would include coded telegrams, reports about meetings, dead-letter box and other clandestine operations, secret audio-surveillance reports, check-up reports and annual reports from the Illegals, etc. As a rule, if they follow all sensible precautionary measures,

Illegals can operate in their target countries normally for up to fifteen or twenty years, in some cases even longer. In the files of ROSA and ROMAN and TREFY were reports from my first boss Colonel Dolzhenko, who ran them before me.

At the very end of the 1980s, General Drozdov ordered Department 3 to train biologist Illegals who were to carry out assignments exclusively for Department 12. In connection with this order, a new, independent group was established in our department. Dolzhenko led this group, which was responsible for the first short-term training assignments of the new 'biology' Illegals, and for their final departure to their countries of long-term residence. Initially, this group had just two staff members – Colonel Dolzhenko and Lieutenant Colonel Duganov – and it reported directly to the chief of Illegal Intelligence, General Drozdov.

All our Illegals were provided with a variety of cover documents to make them invisible to Western counter-intelligence services. Some documents were used only to cross our borders on the way to the country they were being deployed to, through so-called interim countries; other documents were for living in the country of final settlement; yet other documents were for travel to so-called 'third' countries to meet with officers of legal or Illegal *rezidenturas*. A fourth set were documents to be used in case of an urgent recall to Moscow or if the Illegal was in danger of exposure or capture. In such a case, Illegals were supposed to cross at least two or three countries before making their way to Moscow. In every new country they had to cross the border under a new name and with new documents, which were to be used just once. As should be evident, it was practically impossible for enemy counter-intelligence to control or to catch Illegals of Department 12.

Obtaining a Western tertiary education in medicine, biology or a closely related discipline was one of the first and most important operational tasks for our Illegals during their planting period in the countries of settlement. Clearly, to be regarded as credible scientists operating in Western countries, they needed university qualification that would be recognised in the West. Western degrees expanded the Illegals' operational and intelligence possibilities. Just imagine what kind of information could be obtained by a deep-cover secret agent and what sort of special operation or 'direct action' a deep-cover secret agent could help to carry out. For example, as a laboratory assistant or research-scientist in a secret military medical lab; as an employee of a big pharmacological or biotechnological firm experimenting with dangerous pathogens; as a health worker, health inspector or army unit epidemiologist; or as an employee of a state organisation or central government department.

A beginner Illegal codenamed ANVAR was a nondescript man, of middle height, with a quiet voice and balanced demeanour. Before his leaving for the West, at Colonel Dolzhenko's request, I had occasionally managed to operate as a 'dummy' target for ANVAR while we tested him. This role I carried out in the summer and autumn of 1986, not long before his overseas training assignment, or 'staging', in Scandinavia. According to his documents, ANVAR was an inhabitant of one of the Scandinavian countries. He was to get legalised and settle in Sweden. After about three years of successful planting there, ANVAR moved to England and started to carry out assignments for Department 12.

Although our main strength was our Illegals, we also used special agents. Special agents are foreign citizens who are trustworthy, thoroughly checked, and secured by the Russian Foreign Intelligence Service. In this context, 'secured' means that they would come to grief in case of exposure of the documents and information they sent to Moscow.

An agent is moved to the 'special agent' category after a few years of successful work, when the Service has no doubts in him. A change of category for the agent is always followed by additional operational and intelligence training. And work with special agents is very similar to the methods of work with Illegals.

Of all the potential special agents, we were mostly interested in foreign students studying in biological, medical or agricultural faculties of institutes and universities in Russia, those who conscientiously cooperated with the KGB's local intelligence departments. In some ways we duplicated the work of Directorate S's Department 10, i.e. the recruitment of foreign students studying in Russia and using them as support agents for Illegal Intelligence 'abroad'.

I met up with my future agent RIO in Krasnodar in spring 1987. I went there to select prospective young agent-biologists for Department 12 from among some student-foreigners recruited by a local KGB Intelligence unit. RIO was studying at the local university, and specialised in plant virology. He had already been working with the KGB for several years. Our meeting took place in an Inturist hotel, in a large room where the table was set; Lieutenant Colonel Vladimir S., a chief of the local KGB unit, liked grandiose dinners and organised them with all the generosity of a good host.

A dark-haired, handsome young man of average height entered the room. RIO made a nice first impression. He did not try to narrate his opinions; he listened more than he talked. The listening skill is a vital trait for a future agent, one of whose tasks is the ability to know how to gain the trust of strangers. People open up more freely when they see a person is honestly listening to them.

RIO was born in Brazil. His parents moved to Western Europe not long before he began his tertiary education. That suited us, because it meant that RIO could live in Europe after completing his studies. His family ties in Brazil admitted him to the highest level of society there. His uncle was pro-Soviet and it was he who recommended that RIO complete his education in distant Russia.

More than a year before RIO's dispatch to Europe, I collected more information about his relatives in Europe and Brazil. At my request, our colleagues in Krasnodar secretly surveilled almost his every step and organised operational checks on him. I called him to Moscow several times, where in conspiracy apartments RIO learnt how to communicate secretly with the centre. I gave him several secret rendezvous in three European capitals – Berlin, Paris and Lisbon. And one cold and snowy night in January 1989 I accompanied RIO to the Sheremetevo airport.

His long-term assignment included penetration into the Pasteur Institute in France, one of Department 12's main targets in that country, or into one of its affiliated institutes, branches or research laboratories.

This operation was broken into several stages. First we had to decide which country RIO would settle in. He had a choice: he could return to Brazil, or settle in Portugal, a country historically connected with Brazil and his relatives in South America, and become a citizen. I strongly recommended the latter option. The agent's father, who lived in France, also insisted on this, so that he could be close to his son. That was what RIO did.

Portuguese law stated that RIO would have to serve in the country's army. We hoped that service in the army of a NATO nation would provide additional cover for the agent. And we assumed it would also help him to pass whatever loyalty and clearance tests were required when he applied for a job in one of Department 12's targets. Our reasoning was soon vindicated.

After completing a short period of military service in a medical unit, RIO was able to find work in a biological research centre in France that closely collaborated with the Pasteur Institute. In 1990 he became a research scientist in a laboratory experimenting with dangerous human viruses. That was my first major success with RIO, as several years of successful practical research and experimentation there would allow him to continue his work in the Pasteur Institute itself, and would open the possibility of the continuation of his work in military medical laboratories or in research centres which carried out work with military applications.

Counting on long-term work with RIO in the NATO countries and with the possibility of his working in the USA, even at the very start I refused to have any personal contact with him after he left Moscow. Line N Illegal Support officers in the KGB local *rezidenturas* in Lisbon and Paris would help in case of any urgent necessity. Moreover, we did not touch an agent during the first several years in order to quieten any suspicions from hostile counter-intelligence services.

After about two years of peaceful 'planting' the agent was activated, and was given new ways to communicate and a new task. He started to send valuable confidential information about experiments at his research centre. Another of the agent's long-term tasks was to penetrate the small circle of biologists, government and military officials who were closely tied with biological and toxin warfare issues. And if he met with luck, he was himself to become one of those knowledgeable persons. RIO's information about these specialists – their private lives, interests, faults – was important for us.

Influential relatives in Brazil – including his uncle – promised RIO their full support if he was to return home after several years of practice in France. And that was in our interest because we figured that, having received a prestigious position in Brazil after his experience of successful scientific work in Europe, it would make it easier to get him into a department of some objective that interested us in the USA. It was an alluring variant to use RIO against the main enemy.

By this time I was already actively working under a new cover in a joint venture, codenamed CITADEL, that had been organised by Department 12 in three countries of Western Europe, and I was to use CITADEL as cover to continue work with RIO in Europe. But fate managed things differently.

Also quite successful was the settlement and penetration of YAN, another of my agents. He was an ethnic German from Kazakhstan.

One day in 1986, Aliev called me into his office and said, 'Alexander, you and YAN are almost the same age; it will be easier for you both to find a common language. And your interests are likely to be the same too! Work with this case, and you'll be gaining some valuable experience at the same time. Colonel Evgeny Bandura will support, if you're in need.'

I nearly exclaimed, 'Not Bandura!' But I didn't.

When I had studied the agent's case, I saw that the legend for his infiltration was rather simple: marriage of a repatriate ethnic German to a citizen of the German Democratic Republic, i.e. East Germany. The wife, a lecturer at Humboldt University, was a Stasi agent, chosen in 1985 by East German intelligence at our request. The young woman was asked to help naturalise 'a man who was necessary for the Russian comrades', as it was explained by her controllers from Stasi, the East Germany Ministry of State Security. She could only be married to him for two or three years, while he was completing his education at Humboldt University. That was an absolutely indispensable condition of the marriage. YAN's future with the woman from East Germany was not a part of our plans. For us this marriage was only a temporary convenience, a part of the planting and settlement period of agent YAN in the West.

Step by step we then strengthened YAN's cover story – the respectable, promising, medical graduate from East Germany who decided to start a new life in the West. We planned to use him not only for the secret study of Western specialists – medical researchers, biologists and officials – with the goal of their potential recruitment, but also to obtain information about German genetic-engineering research with dangerous human and animal pathogens, and the protective and preventative measures against them that existed in Germany. YAN was to learn the addresses of research laboratories, institutes, centres and military units in the countries of Western Europe that were undertaking covert and secret experiments with recombinant

97

micro-organisms for military purposes, and to develop friendly relationships with their researchers and officials.

As we planned, after several years of living together YAN's marriage of convenience with the Stasi agent broke up. But it did so with a bit of family drama. At first keen only to help in the completion of our task, to aid YAN's naturalisation, the Stasi agent eventually became seriously attracted to him. Knowing that their 'family life' would soon end, the young woman started to demand more attention from YAN. She became anxious if he returned home late, was jealous of his female friends, who were official contacts at the university. When YAN moved out to a separate apartment, she started to pay frequent visits and to demand that he not leave her. Psychological frustrations started to get more and more frequent. And all this was being bugged. It was obvious that the previously lonely, not very attractive older woman wanted desperately to tie YAN to her. We could not take risks with YAN, into whose training and deployment a lot of effort was put. We had to turn to our German colleagues and ask them to 'carry out' the job with their agent, even threaten her if need be. The colleagues evidently knew their work well, for YAN's by then ex-wife quickly left him alone. YAN complained to me later: 'We are quite different people. I don't understand why Evgeny, with whom I worked before you, didn't take this into account. The only good thing out of all of this is that the marriage ended the way Evgeny promised.'

YAN's recall to Moscow before his graduation was simply unavoidable. I thought that the kind of communication with him that had been organised by Colonel Bandura – postcards written in invisible ink from the agent to a 'girl friend' and addressed via the Central Post Office in Moscow – was already unsafe. Moscow, as a postal address for cipher posts and secret writings, was quite an unsecure way of liaising.

After nearly two years of a relationship by correspondence, I met YAN in the conspiracy apartment codenamed GVOZDIKA (about a kilometre from former President Gorbachev's dacha in the Vorobiev hills, on the banks of the Moskva river). He was a typical German: blue eyes, blond hair, self-controlled. In a word, as they said in a well-known Soviet spy-film: 'True Aryan; cold character'. During meetings with YAN, I came to know him better and was reassured by his hard work and goal-oriented attitude. YAN must have found it interesting to talk to me; he was quite friendly, and told me a lot about himself and the town where he was born and grew up, when I consciously evolved onto 'sharp' topics. It seems that Aliev was right when he said that YAN and I would be able to find a common language.

During a month that he spent in Moscow, YAN was taught how to use dead-letter drops, and one-way long-distance communication via ordinary short-wave radio receiver. Starting from that time onwards, he began to receive our ciphers regularly. He answered via secret postal addresses which we organised for him in Western Europe.

His legalisation was carried out successfully. A few years prior to Germany's reunification, YAN finished his medical education at Humboldt University, successfully interned at well-known European medical clinics and hospitals, and received excellent evaluations for his level of practice.

With the aid of Department 12, he opened a private clinic in Germany, using it as a cover to penetrate German professional and scientific circles that were of interest to Department 12. By the beginning of 1992, he was already standing firmly on his own feet; he was making a career as a flourishing physician and had acquired promising contacts for us. I think that from the mid-1990s YAN had to carry out additional tasks. Taking into account that in 1992 Department 12 was amalgamated with the 'sabotage and terror' Department 8, it is likely that, in addition to his normal tasks, he was assigned to uncover the weak points in the biological defences of the countries of Western Europe.

The American Section of Department 12 had several top-class sources in the USA, both agents and Illegals. It seems that from the beginning of the 1980s one of these people operated in the very heart of the American biological warfare programme – possibly either in the US army medical centre in Fort Detrick, or with access to secret information about research carried out in that centre. This source of intelligence information was so vital that it was run by the very head of the American Section, Colonel Leonid Bouz. From time to time he asked me, or Vladimir B—n, to help him plan an intelligence task for, as he said, 'our person from Fort Detrick'. In fact, it was very much because of his information 'about Detrick', as Drozdov remarked once, that Leonid Bouz was made Department 12's leader. And Bouz himself told me that many of his successes were due first and foremost to this man in Detrick.

The importance of this person was so great that meetings with him were made only outside the borders of the USA, mostly in Mexico, Columbia,

Peru and Bolivia, where he could regularly travel for business. This agent sent culture flasks with enclosures – samples of live materials – to Moscow using the urgent VOLNA channel.

Of course, he was not fully trusted, because, within the department, no matter how good the results of an agent's work, ultimately none of us would trust him unconditionally. It is a custom in intelligence, that as the information coming from an agent becomes more important, the more there is speculation about the trustworthiness of the agent. And is the data being supplied *dis*information? Every possible method was used to make sure that a source was not a double agent or working under covert FBI control. The agent was not even left without surveillance in his own house. As a God-obsessed Catholic, our Detrick source had several crucifixes in his house, including one hanging above his bed and another one on the wall in his home office. Captain Mikhail Sh—lov was proud of his idea: 'I suggested making exact copies with spike microphones in them and then covertly replacing the original crosses. Then it would be easy to record from a nearby street, while in the car, what was going on in his house and what he was talking about! It would be enough for a year, and then we'd think of something else!'

An Illegal, who was close to the agent, was to replace the crucifixes with the new ones. He also had to record regularly the information coming from them on a receiver hidden in his car.

In most cases, neither I nor my colleagues from Department 12 knew what kind of biomaterials were coming with each VOLNA delivery. Coded names of agents and Illegals, materials which were obtained by them, names of their covers or their places of work, even the countries of their permanent location, were never identified during the department's regular meetings or annual evaluations; only the general quantity received by each section and the evaluations from the secret laboratories, including those from Biopreparat, and from Directorate T, to which we forwarded 'bio materials'. And they knew only that the material was obtained by 'a unit in the Intelligence Service somewhere overseas', and had been forwarded for their thorough study and practical utilisation. That is all.

But the wider picture could be composited out of bits of information. For example, I could guess exactly what was obtained by each section and what my colleagues were hunting after. Someone would brag about his achievements; someone from among the 'veterans', who was not competent in microbiology, might talk too much when he needed my help with preparation of new assignments for his agents.

For example, the American Section's sources gained information about secret experiments with Rift Valley virus and viral agents which cause Lassa fever, tularaemia and several haemorrhagic fevers, which were carried out, we believed, in medical laboratories of the US Army Medical Research Institute for Infectious Disease (USARMIID) at Fort Detrick, Maryland. Agents who were controlled by Chepornov and Dolzhenko were ordered to obtain the results of experiments with virus vectors, and, in the first instance, about a virus vaccine for smallpox and baculovirus combined with viruses of deadly human fevers. Another order was to procure virus cultures of dengue fever and mosquito-borne viral illnesses.

All of Department 12's geographic sections were in a rush to obtain novel vaccines and antibiotics against the most dangerous diseases caused by pathogenic strains of *Clostridium*, *Salmonella*, *Bacillus*, *Yershinia*, *Shigella*, *Francilla*, and many others, which were developed in secret Western laboratories for their armed forces. The point was that after some genetic modification with these micro-organisms the Soviet and Russian secret army biolabs manufactured novel weaponised strains against which all antidotes, vaccines and antibiotics of the Western armies were useless.

One of the orders for ROSA was to obtain information about the results of experiments with recombinant DNA vaccines, and, ideally, to obtain the materials themselves.

One time Colonel Dolzhenko asked me for help to formulate an order for his sources in England, including the Illegal ANVAR, regarding obtaining information about research on defining the structure, characteristics and molecular mechanisms of several peptide- and receptor-hormones – studies of biochemical mechanisms of the psychology of human beings which can be used to induce unreasoning fear, depression, schizophrenia and other psychological ailments, even death.

Another task for our sources in the USA and Western Europe was to obtain information which might help us to create recombinant strains of anthrax and plague which would produce an enzyme that affects the brain and emotions of the soldiers of an enemy's army. The secret Soviet biolabs were also interested in recombinant micro-organisms able to affect the human immune system.

Towards the end of the 1980s and in the early 1990s it became apparent that the West did not have a real offensive biological warfare programme. Neither did it have the means of delivery for biological weapons, operational plans for their use, nor any effective means of defence against the Soviet (Russian) programme. We found out that although scientific experiments were carried out in the West with dangerous pathogens, their aim was to develop defences against the well-known types of biological warfare.

We discovered that, at the time, Western countries were absolutely unprepared to face our weapons if the Soviet Union (or, later, Russia) had started a biological war against the main enemy, the USA and the NATO countries.

Starting from the end of the 1980s, Department 12 began actively to use the channel of legal immigration – the massive flow of immigrants who travelled from the republics of the Soviet Union to the West – to dispatch our agents to different countries. According to the immigration laws of many Western countries – and this remains the case even now – the first preference in admissions was, as a rule, given to young specialists with university degrees: for example, research-scientists, sanitary and environmental health professionals, ecologists, biologists and the like – that is, people with technical training. Such specialists are in high demand in most capitalist countries. So we started to create a 'second echelon' – autonomous networks of auxiliary agents in addition to our main weapons, Illegals and special agents. It was one of the elements of a new strategic initiative of Department 12 in Western Europe and the USA, begun during the 1990s and implemented step by step.

Among this category of agent, our European Section first singled out ethnic Greeks and Germans, who were more active in attempts to return to their historical homelands than were other groups. I got access to and checked long lists of ethnic Greeks and Germans who had applied for immigration visas in embassies in Moscow. That information was accumulated by KGB counter-intelligence and its successors. In order not to miss a single valuable person, I sifted through the lists accumulated by the Lubyanka. I was first of all interested in KGB agents with biological, medical, veterinary and agricultural education, and also dentists, massage therapists, and even hair-dressers – people with 'practical' professions, i.e. those who, with our support, could open up private practices in the West. I selected about twenty candidates.

The Greek and German ethnic émigrés interested us for a number of reasons. First, Greece and Germany are NATO countries and members of the European Union. Second, in Greece, counter-intelligence surveillance of repatriates was not as strict as in other countries of the European Union. Greece offered quite pleasant conditions for fast settlement and integrating new migrants into its society. After a year and a half, the recent immigrant was already a Greek citizen with full rights and was able to move around the European Union without visa and in complete freedom. And to move freely to other countries of the world.

Here I must say that I soon became convinced that even this relatively unreliably 'secured' agent network could be quite effective.

So I seized the opportunity to create and use the network of auxiliary agents in Western Europe. I believed that, most likely, the value of intelligence information obtained by this kind of agent would not be high. But why dismiss the other possibilities? Such agents could well be used to carry out separate tasks – for example, by obtaining information about objectives and specialists of interest to Department 12, and by penetrating objectives as technical workers and administrative employees, even if the agents did not have any medical or biological education. Or even by using them for combat operations, such as placing small containers of dangerous microorganisms and deadly toxins into preselected drops close to targets, in order to knock them off line or to destroy them in the event of a large-scale military conflict or war. To sum up, we would use the agents at once to carry out acts of sabotage and terrorism if the situation called for it. I explained all of these benefits in detail to Department 12 in a memorandum to General Drozdov. He agreed with this suggestion.

The Greek group, which I assembled gradually, comprised, mostly, females. With our help, the principal agent of the group, RAIMOND, opened a private trading company and soon became an associate of several firms in Greece, Cyprus and France. Her numerous close contacts among respected businessmen of those countries enabled us to get access to serious secret intelligence information. Furthermore, her frequent business trips to other West European countries allowed us to use her to handle containers with biological materials received from our sources in Europe.

Although cautioned not to hurry events, RAIMOND could not abstain from the temptation to make a quick fortune; she was too reckless. She soon moved into financial speculation, and she also helped to transfer large sums of money through Moscow and St Petersburg banks overseas. Then she developed a close relationship with a Greek, Georgious K., who was actively being sought by Interpol for supplying arms to the regimes of dictators in North Africa and the Near East. Because I left the Service about that time, I do not know if their co-operation was an operational or intelligence necessity or not. But it seems that some shady operation cost RAIMOND her head; in the summer of 1994, RAIMOND and her children were shot dead in the agent's summer cottage near Athens. Was this a result of her dangerous business connections, or did she know too much?

With the help of ANGEL, another member of the Greek group, we got access to documents of the regional police department in Komotini.

The first operational assignment I gave to ANGEL was to open a beauty salon. I reasoned that among the agent's clients there might be people who would interest us. But I could not predict just how successful the agent's new life would be.

A single and attractive young woman, she immediately caught the attention of local men. Moreover, she caught the attention of the police chief. He started to demand private meetings with her. Apart from counter-espionage functions, the police chief registered deaths and marriages, and issued personal identifications, birth certificates, and passports. Thus, we had a brilliant opportunity to document new Illegals! Everything was quite easy. My agent became a lover of the police chief. The other things came to us as easily as a knuckle twitch, almost like a stereotyical spy novel.

With the help of a Line N Illegal Support officer in the Athens *rezidentura*, we restored contacts with two 'sleeping agents' codenamed ELLA and EMMA. Thanks to successful marriages to quite wealthy Greeks, they came into close contact with influential Greek businessmen, including those who had business ties with large pharmacological companies in Western Europe, with their own branches and affiliated companies in various countries of the world.

The only man in the Greek group, agent YURI, was offered the role of radio operator. His cover as owner of a radio repair shop in Athens was highly suitable.

The flow of German expatriates was so active, and there were so many interesting variants, that I handed the whole 'German channel' over to my colleague Major Valery K., who controlled Department 12's work in all German-speaking countries of Europe. Valery actively immersed himself in the work and soon created another agent network.

The successful experience of the European Section, in planting auxiliary agents into target countries through legal immigration, soon led the department's other sections to try their hands at it. For example, the Asian Section actively placed agents who were ethnic Turks, Uzbeks, Koreans and Chinese; the American Section worked with Armenians and Russian Jews. Within the first two years of the 1990s Department 12 deployed about twenty such prospective agents into target countries for long-term settlement.

All of the agents who were dispatched through the legal immigration channel were supplied with permanent means of communication, including meetings and dead-letter drops. The agents were given long-term assignments to be worked on during the resettlement period. Each of them had personal allotted tasks and was given two-way post channels of communication through covert addresses. That was how we received information about their planting and settlement, and about their progress in making valuable contacts in their new societies. We arranged one or two direct contacts every two years. Also, we received detailed reports from them and ordered each of them to keep strictly to their instructions during the first phase of planting in the host communities. We supported them with money, ten or more thousand American dollars per year for each agent.

The trustworthiness of agents and even of Illegals is a constant worry for Directorate S. It has never placed total trust in its people, especially those who remain overseas for a long time. The more successful their operations, and the more valuable the information they obtain, the more suspicions are kept up about them. What if the source is a double agent? What if he or she is under the control of the enemy's counter-intelligence service? As for special agents, we were even more dubious, suspecting them of working for two masters just as double agents do. Only when we received really priceless material exposing important state secrets did we come to any firm conclusion as to the value of our Illegals and secret agents. We were therefore obliged to check them every two to three years.

In short, the general principle of such checks was that each checked person received a false (dummy) mission masquerading as a real and very important one. Of course, every aspect of the assignment was under our control and observation.

Directorate S's Department 9 checked all operational files to uncover disinformation. Mathematicians working in this department used specially designed computer programs to sift the accumulated data received from our Illegals and agents, and even from officers operating in KGB *rezidenturas*.

Sooner or later in the testing, psychotropic drugs were applied. We used special pharmacological products, for example SP-17, developed in a secret KGB laboratory. This drug induces in a person a feeling of boundless trust in his companions and an unsuppressed desire to answer thoroughly all questions, share even the most secret concealed innermost thoughts and wishes – in short, all that which, in a normal state, a person would never reveal. This 'remedy which loosens the tongue' has no taste, no smell, no colour, and no known immediate side effects. And, most important, a person has no recollection of having had the 'heart-to-heart' talk. This testing method was widely used, especially during the period of Illegals' development and training, and when they returned from their first overseas training assignments. SP-17 might also be administered during Illegals' short trips to Moscow for holidays. In almost all the operational files of Illegals and special agents of Department 12 which I ran or had access to, I found evidence of the use of SP-17.

These operations were always held in conditions where there were no distractions. Department 12 carried them out in operational conspiracy apartments, usually in Moscow or East Berlin. Officers of the department invited the Illegal or other agent for a friendly dinner 'among our own people' and a grandiose drinking of spirits. At a suitable moment, SP-17 was administered, mixed into the contents of one of the bottles. In order to avoid an accidental overdose, and to control the condition of the 'drunkard' (i.e. the secretly interrogated person), there was always – either in the adjacent room or among the actual 'warm, friendly company' – a medical doctor to neutralise the 'medicine' quickly. If, later on, the interrogated person still tried to recall why he so quickly became drunk, he was shown 'evidence' of the 'wild party' – empty bottles in profusion, sufficient to prove they were drunk all night. We found and used a few other situations in which we could secretly apply the drug – in the sauna, while picnicking, etc. – and, in those circumstances, the episode of 'sleepiness' could be explained as sun stroke, intoxication from the fumes, hot weather, fatigue, etc.

Odd things happened on occasion. I remember one case when the officer controlling the operation himself had so much vodka that he forgot the questions and answers. Instead, on the cassette of the 'heart-to-heart talk' with the interrogated person we heard the officer's own frank confessions.

In only one case known to me did an agent suspect something. Not long before RIO was sent to Portugal, the head of Department 12 insisted that SP-17 be used as an additional check on him. Major Vasily L. – the future support officer for RIO in France – took part in the test, but Vasily came on too fast, questioning before the drug started to work. In addition, instead of me, my colleague Major Valery K. (a former doctor and a psychiatrist) was sent to the meeting.

Later RIO complained to me, when we were alone: 'Why was Vasily in such a hurry? How come he kept pouring more and more alcohol into me? And I think he asked me some weird questions. And he demanded that I tell him something. Now I can't recall everything. I think he slipped some muck into my drink.'

What could I say to him? That it could have been me pouring him drinks in Vasily's place? Our profession is one of the most cynical in the world.

Psychotropic drugs were also used on our own officers whose loyalty was under suspicion. They were used when the Service interrogated Major Gennady Varenik. I know that psychotropic drugs were also used in the case of Colonel Vitaly Yurchenko after his successful 'action-movie escape' from the CIA's control after his fake defection in August 1985, in Italy. Apparently, the heads of the Service feared that in his several months with the CIA, Yurchenko might have been recruited as a double agent. I recall his grey, puffy face as he strolled on the centre's asphalt paths during lunchtimes in 1986. He walked with restraint, only nodding his head as a greeting to acquaintances. On his jacket shone his recent award – the Order of the Red Star, given to him for the successful completion of the 'infiltration operation'. The Service does not even trust its heroes.

Using special remedies from the arsenal of Directorate S's secret laboratories, we would also warn or punish agents who wanted to end collaboration with us. Such warnings implied that a more severe punishment might be in store. Among the weapons were chemical compounds that left a strong, disgusting smell, and provoked vomiting, headaches and other unpleasant involuntary physiological reactions.

Once Colonel Aliev transferred to me the case of an agent who had been deployed into West Germany in the early 1980s. The agent, a medical doctor, had been dispatched to the West through ethnic Jewish emigration channels and had been successfully settled – with our financial help – into a private medical practice, a psychotherapy clinic. Among his clients were professionals who interested Department 12. Thanks to his promising start and the contacts he had made, the agent was able to widen his intelligence possibilities.

Studying the agent's files, I saw that for two or three years he had been avoiding regular contacts and had missed scheduled rendezvous with us, and where he had attended, he had come by circuitous means. Having experienced freedom and smelled good money from his own private practice, the agent clearly desired to avoid communicating with us. In order to make him reactivate his work and continue his co-operation with us, it was decided to frighten him.

Before contemplating the use of special chemicals – malodorous preparations – a Line N officer of the KGB *rezidentura* in Bonn masqueraded as a normal patient and visited the agent's clinic, to suss out his premises to find out where 'special chemicals' would have the greatest effect. Soon the 'patient' visited the clinic again. This time, everything that he could surreptitiously treat the officer sprayed with a small can provided from the centre – the front door handle, the carpet in the waiting room and the hallway, and even some of the furniture and the wall near the entrance were sprayed. Before an hour had passed, our perfume had started to act. No amount of carpet cleaning, furniture replacement, or washing of the floor and walls could rid the office of the disgusting smell. The renegade agent lost clients for a long time and had to close down his practice. He was so frightened that he moved to another city, where he attempted to hide. He was found even there. Nevertheless, after several meetings we decided to drop contact with him, because the agent was so frightened and demoralised that he was of no use. He feared everything, and everywhere he went he had hallucinations of the long arm of Moscow.

And now let's sum up and answer the question: just how many Illegals – deep-penetration professionals – valuable special agents and other agents could have worked for the amalgamated 'biological' department in the 1990s? By the beginning of the 1990s the tasks of Department 12 were actively carried out by about ten Illegals in North America, Western Europe and in the countries of South-East Asia. At the start of the 1990s another five Illegals were being placed. All of them had to operate in English and German-speaking countries. When Department 8 was absorbed into the structure of Department 12, we added about ten more Illegals. They were trained to plan, prepare and carry out acts of sabotage and terrorist acts in enemy territory. So, during the 1990s there were about twenty-five Illegals in the amalgamated 'biological' department. Valuable and special agents – Western citizens – added another twenty or so sources in target countries. By adding fifteen or twenty migrant agents, I assume about sixty people carried out Department 12's tasks overseas in the 1990s, and possibly as many still do so today. It is an impressive number, if you consider the kind of clandestine tasks they had to carry out!

Can you imagine such power, the humungous strength of the Russian Foreign Intelligence Service, being abandoned just because of detente and democratisation? Would all the efforts and money expended in training and developing our people be forgotten? Would all our agents be stood down and the Illegals recalled just because Russia was taking part in the next round of biological weapons talks in Geneva? I wouldn't bet on it.

Apparently, the Western world can't bring itself to believe to what extent it is transparent and vulnerable to Russian Illegal Intelligence. Directorate S, as well as its army brother-in-arms – the Illegal Intelligence Directorate of the GRU – represents the greatest threat to the safety of Western society. Directorate S is able to carry out all its assignments overseas, even during political and military crises in the target countries, and to deliver regularly secret intelligence from countries where there are no official Russian representatives. Directorate S is able to operate even when all 'legal' *rezidenturas* find themselves under the strict control of local counter-intelligence services.

Directorate S uses its specific intelligence methods and works differently than other directorates of the Service. It is the only one in the Forest which is able to extract secrets from the enemy without even using foreign agents.

If Directorate S is really interested in a valuable foreigner – a person who knows important government secrets – then it makes sure that it does everything that it can, so that this person is persuaded to co-operate with the Service. Major work always comes before the recruitment pitch. An 'objective of cultivation' would notice nothing suspicious. All his or her friends, relatives, relations are the same as ever. Nothing obvious is done. No Russian from the embassy or a trade delegation persistently tries to become a 'friend'. Nobody displays any sudden interest in him or his family. Nobody asks unusual questions about colleagues; nobody shows interest in what work he or she is undertaking. But Illegal Intelligence has already gathered all possible information about the 'objective', even biographical facts which that person might already have forgotten or does not want to remember. Someone from among the agents or the Illegals (for some good reason) will have already visited a university where he studied, a town or city where he worked, and carefully sought to learn whether the candidate agent has any problems or not. Is he able to keep his tongue behind his teeth or does he blab confidences after a glass of wine; is he a womaniser; gay? Who are his close friends and is there among them anyone with access to state secrets and intelligence information? If yes, then what are their names, addresses, habits, favourite holiday places, their wives' names, their lovers', who are their personal physicians, taxi-drivers, masseurs, etc.? It is hard to list everything! When the study transforms into the final stages – cultivation and the recruitment proposition – then, among contacts or friends from the club, there will be a charming woman or man, who will have the same interests, will do a good turn, help to solve some vital worry or problem. Basically, it will be a kind, charismatic, sympathetic, understanding, intelligent person. He or she will have the documents and the biography of a citizen of the candidate's country, or be a citizen of an allied country. But in reality he or she is really a deep-cover Russian agent who has successfully penetrated what is to us a hostile community under an assumed name and using someone else's biography.

Directorate S practically never uses compromise or blackmail in order to win over a foreigner. A person has to work for Russian Intelligence of his own free will. If he is a pacifist, then that is a good thing! We can play on that. If he likes money, that's not bad either. If he feels he is a loser at work, that is quite suitable as well. Everything is added to the accumulation of facts, everything is thoroughly examined, in order to figure out which type of development will be most suitable, which soft spots should be played on.

If the person could be very valuable to Russian Illegal Intelligence but does not show any love or strong sympathy for Russia or its people, then Department S uses a refined variant such as 'false flag' recruitment. The 'help' would be asked for in the name of a more suitable organisation.

Directorate S uses its top 'aerobatic skills' when recruiting in the name of another country's secret intelligence service, or in the name of a terrorist or extremist organisation. For such serious operations Directorate S usually uses its Special Reserve, which is a key part of Department 1. Officers of that department are former Illegals, career professionals, who, after lengthy years of overseas work, were recalled to Moscow and assigned to the staff of Directorate S in order to carry out the most important assignments.

In the case of recruitment in the name of Western intelligence services, terrorist or extremist organisations, 'the target' is not able to find out that in reality he or she has agreed to work for Russian Intelligence, rather than for Interpol, MOSSAD, MI6 or the CIA, etc., under which names the person might have been approached 'for help'. Through all the years of their 'co-operation', Directorate S would continue to preserve the source's belief that he or she is being controlled by people from Jerusalem, London or Washington, and not from the Moscow Centre.

Not all Russians are drunks and fools as they are portrayed in Hollywood movies. Even though on many occasions Russia was a country thought to be on the verge of losing its power, it always rose from the ashes. Since the collapse of the Soviet Union, Western democracies have not taken the Russian Foreign Intelligence Service as a serious threat. But the mechanism of deep penetration into Western societies has continued, with new opportunities opened by *perestroika*, its consequences and 'new global thinking'. Let's not forget that in 1992 the Russian Foreign Intelligence Service was making major personnel and money investments for espionage on biological warfare issues.

Chapter 6

Making Our People Invisible

Intelligence work has one moral law – it is justified by results.
JOHN LE CARRÉ, *THE SPY WHO CAME IN FROM THE COLD*

E ach Illegal had to have his or her own new false persona and received strict individual training. We had a saying: 'Our Illegals are goods sold by the piece!' This underlined the uniqueness of the department's Illegals. It is quite impossible to list all the numerous versions and types of Illegal training and documentation. That would require a separate book.

Department 12 worked closely with Departments 2 and 3. Department 2 took care of 'paperwork' – that is, it provided Illegals with documents and names. Other departments could also acquire necessary documents if they had proper agent and operational opportunities. Department 3 selected candidates, trained them and dispatched them overseas.

In the overwhelming majority of cases, Illegals were supplied with genuine documents obtained by Department 2. Any official papers – birth, marriage, divorce and death certificates, including deaths in traffic and other accidents, other personal information, such as, for example, addresses and biographical data on genuine and potential relatives – all this had essential meaning for Department 2. All of it was hoarded, as there could be further use for such material. Sooner or later the bits and pieces, facts and documents that were gained, were analysed, selected, sorted and processed in order to document and develop Illegals' covers and life stories.

Department 2 recruits agents who are able to obtain genuine identity documents. In my time, the most valuable of such agents were considered to be church devotees, officers of visa and passport registration sections, employees of internal affairs' departments and archives, police, customs and border control officers – anyone at all who had access to the processing of driving licences, passports, certificates, certified copies of IDs and other official specimens of personal and other documents. The perfect situation is one in which the agent can obtain blank passports or birth, death or marriage certificates. When reading or watching the news, whenever you see a case of corruption – it could be the selling of blank passports, birth certificates, or other IDs by officials for kickbacks – think about whether this might be a sign of the activity of Illegal Intelligence. Agents who can, if necessary under oath, confirm the 'fact' of their acquaintance with a certain person, the one for whom Illegal Intelligence is assembling documentation, are also very valuable. For example, the 'real fact' of their having both been at a college, institute or university, or having lived in the same town, or having been on holiday in the same resort, etc., is worthwhile when it comes to falsifying documents. Ideally, such agents collaborate on ideological grounds rather than for money. Only in exceptional circumstances is blackmail used to motivate an unwilling agent. Believing that fear of exposure is not a reliable basis for secret collaboration, Directorate S doesn't usually use that type of compelled recruitment.

It's impossible within the framework of my book to mention all the varieties of documentation and detail the development of Illegals' covers and life stories. The most secure one is the identity of a dead person.

The most tempting kinds of documentation were those which became available when Department 2 managed to acquire birth and death certificates of an orphan who died as a child or a baby. The most attractive cases were when the child died far from its motherland and did not have close relatives. Birth certificates of children who have only distant and long forgotten relatives are also interesting. However cynical it sounds, it was considered a big success for us when Department 2 managed to obtain children's birth certificates after a whole family died in a traffic or other kind of accident. Wedding certificates of couples who died or were killed accidentally soon after their marriage are also interesting. Why, for example, could those newly weds not have had a child? The documentation department could use such a marriage certificate to develop a cover story for an Illegal who was supposedly born from their marriage.

Colonel Ismail Aliev had extensive experience in obtaining documents. Before he was promoted to the post of Deputy Chief of Department 12, he worked in Department 2. Whichever country he operated in, his favourite places for strolls were local cemeteries. Consequently his safes in overseas KGB stations were packed with 'the deceased' – the result of his walks and the contacts he made with cemetery keepers.

Aliev acquired genuine documents and copies of birth, death and marriage certificates, medical insurances policies, driver's licences. He even photographed gravestones. All these could be used as the sources of facts for future covers and life stories for Illegals. My colleague Captain Yury E. from Department 8 was not so lucky. During his tour of duty to Australia he tried to recruit a cemetery keeper near Canberra. He failed and local counterintelligence quickly traced his contacts with the cultivated 'objective', then quietly expelled Captain E. from the country without declaring him *persona non grata*.

A real person has died, but his name and his potential life story are now in the hands of Illegal Intelligence. This fabricated and non-existent phantom continues his life, acts, occupies space in our real world, and even has a family. And this man may have children who do not suspect that they have been born to the already dead.

Illegals have also used the identification of people who are alive, but that option is used rarely, as it is not entirely secure. The IDs of living persons could be used for an Illegal's infiltration into another country, to cross the border, and also for an urgent escape from a country where he is operating. Such use of a living peron's ID might occur with the real owner's consent or without it.

In the first case a foreign citizen – our agent – gives his passport to the Service for a certain period of time while he is secretly being transferred to Russia. The Service takes care to hide the agent's absence in his homeland. In Russia he or she lives under total and vigilant control and under the protection of Illegal Intelligence. Sometimes, an innocent foreign citizen whose name was secretly used by us didn't even suspect the existence of his double. Such was the case of the Illegals Igor and Natalia Lyuskov, who were documented as citizens of the United Kingdom under the real names of James Peatfield and Anna Marie Nemeth. These Illegals were arrested with British passports during their training assignment in Western Europe in 1992. For us, an Illegal's failure was a rare and extraordinary event, which was always subjected to thorough examination; the Service's professionalism was affected!

A husband-and-wife team of Illegals, Elena and Dmitry Olshevksy, were arrested in Canada in 1996 and sent back to Moscow in 1998. In Toronto, they lived under the names of Ian and Laurine Lambert. According to the official version, they applied for Canadian passports and thereby alerted the Canadian authorities, who hauled them off to jail.

One particular aspect of the Olshevsky case interested me: how did Canadian counter-intelligence discover their Russian origins? In case of arrest, every Illegal has a back-up legend. In the case of the Olshevsky-Lamberts, it probably took the following form: 'Yes, we did use a false identity. We're very sorry, and we apologise, but our circumstances made us do it. Both of us, back in our motherland [here they mention any Western country, but not Russia], had family or personal problems. [For example, a loveless or broken marriage, a marriage opposed by relatives, minor legal differences, drug addiction, etc.] But we love each other, so we decided to make a break with the past and rebuild our lives – to leave our country, change our names, and start a new life from scratch. And the Canadian birth certificates? We bought them.'

An Illegal learns his or her back-up legend thoroughly during training. It is very hard for the police and counter-intelligence to crack it, because the key 'facts' can be verified by 'witnesses' – supporting agents of Russian Illegal Intelligence. Most often, the legend is accepted, and the worst thing that may happen to an Illegal is his expulsion from the country. In this case, the Illegal remains available for further operations in the West: the Moscow Centre simply gives him a new identity, new documents, a new cover story, and a new task.

The Olshevskys' case was trickier. I don't think they were betrayed by any of Directorate S's defectors. If that had been the case, then they would have been arrested years earlier, and not while applying for Canadian passports. It is more likely to have been the result of something more radical. Perhaps there was a mole in Directorate S, an agent of Western intelligence, who had access to Illegals' files, and the Olshevskys' application for passports was simply used by Canadian counter-intelligence as a useful opportunity to seize them. Alternatively, perhaps a vigilant Canadian counter-intelligence officer found a hole in 'Ian's' and 'Laurine's' story and didn't believe their 'genuine' Canadian birth certificates.

When the capture of the 'Lamberts' was announced, my wife remembered the Olshevskys, with whom she had studied at the same university. She recalled that their rash marriage had surprised fellow students at the time. Elena and Dmitry were very different people, were never friends, and weren't romantically involved. This artificial marriage can be explained by the fact that, at the time, the Intelligence Service was training the Olshevskys as a husband-and-wife team, but didn't pay much attention to their psychological compatibility. It seems that psychologists of Directorate S's Department 3 thought this wasn't too much of a problem, and relied too heavily on their past experience of Illegals training – i.e. that, with time, their differences would be worked out, and they'd grow closer through their working partnership. But it seems that these two just didn't fit together. In the end, this was probably the major cause of their failure. When the Olshevskys returned to Russia, they divorced.

Sometimes circumstances called for slight, barely noticeable corrections to be inserted into a genuine passport – the date of birth, a letter in the last name, etc. This kind of work was performed by the Operational Technical Department of Directorate S. Paper, ink, glue, paper clips, hidden security details – all, without exception, could be perfectly copied by that department. As officers of the Operational Technical Department pointed out, even the most modern analytical methods of detecting forged documents, including gas chromatography, luminescence photography, nuclear magnetic resonance, etc., were not able to expose one of their skilfully 'corrected' genuine passports. 'This is child's play. There are ink and stamp copies of practically all important official organisations of the target countries in our collection at the Lubyanka!' officers of that department assured me when I needed cover documents.

The Illegals Directorate can perfectly process passports of any country of the world, although our Illegals used these 'corrected' passports on extremely rare occasions, for example when a cover story needed to be changed, or to escape from a country when several borders needed to be crossed before reaching Moscow. But in either case, the Illegal was always searching for the possibility of exchanging his Moscow-made passport for one issued in the West.

The officers of Department 2 were always away on trips. Using numerous covers, such as, for example, a Russian businessman, Australian farmer, Polish photographer – it would be hard to enumerate them all – they crossed the borders of many countries. The aim of their trips was to gather information about passport control and to discover where an Illegal could cross a border without suspicion.

Until recently, in many Western countries there wasn't any strict control over the issuing of many kinds of ID. But this unwillingness of a large part of Western society to identify itself properly unintentionally works in favour of the Russian Illegal Intelligence. For example, in some Commonwealth states up till recent times it was unnecessary to have photos on driving licences. Also licences, even passports, could be obtained through the post without visiting police or other authorisation offices.

Each Illegal can possess several IDs with different names. As a custom, the *rezident* who controls several Illegals and special agents has the most IDs.

The slightest mistake or miscalculation in the Illegal's documentation can result in damaging consequences which cannot be repaired. I was a witness to one such case, when a 'not thorough enough' operation to obtain a British passport, by using a birth certificate in the name of a New Zealander who had died as a child, led to the arrest of Anvar Kadyrov, who had been deployed to New Zealand for his settlement and establishment. A genuine New Zealand birth certificate had been acquired by Department 2 and used for the cover documentation of the Illegal. But MI5, the British counter-intelligence service, found out that the passport had been requested in the name of a dead person. It appears that Department 2 had counted too much on the lack of a systematic archive for the registration of both births and deaths in New Zealand. They had also underestimated the skills and experience of the local counter-intelligence service. Due to Kadyrov's arrest, his Illegal Support officer Major Valery M., who operated in New Zealand under diplomatic cover, was expelled. I met Valery in the centre's cafeteria. I myself had just returned to Moscow after assignment to Frankfurt-am-Main in West Germany. Valery was angered and dishevelled. As we used to say, he had been 'burnt', and was no longer able to work in any *rezidenturas*. He swore with the full range of his vocabulary at Directorate S and Department 2, and the country of New Zealand and its people, which he had underestimated. That case was scrupulously investigated in Directorate S. In order to make sure other Illegals were better protected against failure, both General Drozdov and his successor, Colonel Yuri Zhuravlev, always tried to derive whatever lessons they could from such catastrophes.

Labour and time expended by Directorate S's Department 3 during the selection and training of candidate Illegals were enormous. Officers of Department 3 were constantly overloaded with operational files on their candidates. Offices were overcrowded, with as many as five or six people huddled together in a room. This department had the biggest staff working undercover in tertiary institutions. They selected candidates among students.

Enormous efforts were made to select only the few young people with real prospects for success from among hundreds of potential candidates. A special group of Department 3 psychologists studied candidates' temperaments and characters to select those best suited for clandestine work overseas, i.e. those who would be able to overcome loneliness and long-term isolation from their families left behind in the homeland, who would be able to overcome the monotony of an outwardly unnoteworthy life full of deliberate self-denial and self-sacrifice, and who would be able to blend into their surroundings and be patient. By using special psychological training and methods of psychotherapy, Department 3's psychologists taught candidates skills which would help them to face a hostile society into which they should not only 'dissolve' but in which they had to carry out the tasks and orders of the Moscow Centre.

It is very important for an Illegal, as a beginner in the target country, to acquire the habits and the lifestyle of its citizens quickly; to learn to dress the way that is 'normal' in that society; to learn how to open bank accounts, use credit cards and cheque books, hire a vehicle, rent an apartment, a room in a hotel or a motel, make purchases in a shop, etc. To sum up, to learn how to be more like everyone else. One of the main commandments of an Illegal is do not stand out; be as imperceptible as possible. To break that rule threatens exposure and inevitable failure.

Frederick Forsyth, in his book *The Day of the Jackal*, writes in detail about documentation used by an assassin to obtain a false identity so as to facilitate killing President de Gaulle. Despite having no intelligence background, Forsyth describes some of the same methods of documentation and legislation as are used by Directorate S for its Illegals. I read this book in English while I was a cadet of the Andropov Red Banner Intelligence Institute, but it also began to be translated into Russian at the same time, and was being serialised in a Soviet popular magazine. Suddenly, its publication had ceased. It seems that the KGB became alarmed – what if Soviet readers used the same methods as Forsyth's main character to escape from the country, or, even worse, to kill a member of the Soviet elite?

Once or twice a year we met with retired Illegals, bringing our families, in one of Department 12's conspiracy apartments. A large table with all sorts of goodies was set up in one room; in the next – us, our wives and an invited Illegal 'who'd come in from the cold'. These informal meetings helped us to understand better the lifestyles our Illegals endured while living in the host country to carry out our assignments.

I remember one meeting especially well. This happened during the winter of 1990 in our conspiracy apartment in Moscow centre, not so far from the metro station Mayakovskaya.

In one room I saw pictures on the walls of the Illegal commonly called Rudolf Abel. If a person is talented, he is talented in everything! That legendary Illegal was also an amazing artist. In another room a table was set for our children. During that evening we met with retired Illegals Galina and Mikhail Fedorov. They had served forty years in Illegal Intelligence. For fifteen of those forty years they worked in a French-speaking country of Western Europe. A sensible pair, they sat with us at the table and shared their reflections.

'Once we were urgently called into the centre. Why was it such an urgent matter? We do not know, and it was not the custom to ask such questions. Of course, in this case we had an urgent channel running through Belgium, Italy, then Turkey and finally to Moscow. In order for our unexpected departure not to look suspicious, we passed the word around to our neighbours and the clients of our small firm, our cover, that we had decided to take a holiday along the Mediterranean.

'We arrived in Moscow and stayed in a conspiracy apartment without going outside for all of that time – we were training to use new forms of communications. Then it was time to return and we suddenly realised! We were as pale as spirochaetes! Who would believe that we had spent three weeks in Italy under the August summer sun? Our superiors rushed us to the airport and sent us all the way to the Crimea for three days to tan. We were sunburned beyond belief! We came back home with peeling noses and overcooked skin. Our neighbours kept asking us for the hotel in which we stayed, where we had such a "lovely holiday".'

This pair of Illegals helped the Soviet government to solve the problem of the Caribbean crisis in 1962. Extremely important secret information passed through their hands from valuable agents of Illegal Intelligence about NATO's plans of pre-emptive atomic strikes against the Soviet Union in the event of war, and NATO's tactical operations in Europe.

Our candidates learnt all of their spy-craft in Moscow during their training period, while living in operational apartments. There they were immersed into the atmosphere of the target country's society, created for them by Department 3. They listened to music and radio programmes, watched movies and television shows which were then popular overseas. They perfected their foreign languages. They had to master the dialects of the country where they were to live for a certain time – usually a few years – before transferring to the country of permanent residence.

Overseas preliminary training assignments – *stazhirovky* – preceding final placement in the West are the Illegals' first combat assignments. The *stazhirovka* is an essential, controlled and final check of a new Illegal's abilities to undertake operational and intelligence work under deep cover abroad.

Usually the 'run-in' lasts from a few weeks to several months. As a rule, during that time several main operational tasks are undertaken. First of all, the reliability of the Illegal's cover story and documents is checked.

An Illegal (or Illegals, if they are placed simultaneously as a husband-and-wife team) is given training assignments which take him or her through several countries. It is good when travel documents bear stamps for border crossing; an old passport provokes less suspicion. Moreover, the recent stamps and visas are useful for study by the Technical Section of Directorate S's Department 2. For example, Illegals of Directorate S's Special Reserve, who carry out extremely important tasks, frequently need the most up-to-date documents to disguise their identities.

Another objective of the training assignment is to reinforce a cover story developed in the centre with new and old true facts, so an Illegal can convincingly and plausibly relate to his or her supposed past. In this way possible gaps in an Illegal's cover story can be filled in.

New elements of a life story could, for example, be short-term relationships and neutral contacts. Some neutral contacts might be very useful in an Illegal's future clandestine work. An Illegal's short-term stays may be in those specific places where a person whose notional life-story documents the Illegal carries might live, study and work.

We used such cover-story reinforcements as short-term studies in Western universities, institutes or professional training courses (e.g. in therapeutic massage, computer programming, environmental health and science, engineering and business courses dealing with environmental management, etc.). Real certificates of completion can always be referred to later. It's good if an Illegal has a photo of his graduation. To reinforce the legend of his residence in some specific place for a certain period which is not quite convincingly covered by Department 2's selected 'facts', an Illegal can use photographs of his notional 'friends' obtained by the department. This was done by Department 12 quite often, for example by using amateur photos of 'friends and acquaintances', 'school friends' or 'your own' graduation class to pass for one of the young people in the group photos. Naturally, an Illegal has to use such photographs with great care and should not refer to them unless it is necessary. In any case, at the initial deployment into a host country, which follows the staging, these loans could work.

During run-ins we recommended that Illegals stay in rented apartments or in average-size hotels where the owners don't demand personal identification (unlike bigger, fashionable hotels, which prize their reputations). Taking into account all of the above, Line N Illegal Support officers of local *rezidenturas* or Illegals in the field took part in preparing training routes for the new Illegals. They studied conditions and living regimes of hotels, camping grounds, motels, lodges, etc.

In small hotels, private motels, hostels, campsites and lodges it is easier to pose as a traveller, foreign student or researcher while perfecting one's language skills. Or to gather material in a local university for a research project or to write a book. Or to pose as a freelance of some kind engaged in literary work.

The owners or landlords will most likely remember the polite, modest, well-mannered and serious young man or woman and supply a positive opinion and reference if needed. And that would be a real or, as we used to say, 'reinforcing' fact in an Illegal's cover story.

Apart from that, the addresses of average-size hotels, motels, lodges, campsites, etc. are safer to use as temporary return post addresses. Our Illegals could use them to inform us about their movements, training routes, border crossings, and completed assignments if postal communication was assigned with our agreement. This channel – a letter or a card to a secret postal address – is normally recommended in cities and regions where there are always many tourists, transit passengers, students on holiday, or a large flow of seasonal workers. The 'letter boxes' (the secret postal addresses) are normally situated in a third country. Their keepers are almost always Illegals or specially trusted agents. At the beginning of the 1990s we started to use secret coded computer communication with Illegals.

Another task of the preliminary training assignment is to check an Illegal's ability to select independently places for future clandestine contacts with our local *rezidenturas* through dead drops and momentary contacts, and to use short- and long-distance radio communication with Moscow.

I think that, at present, despite Directorate S's use of various modern electronic communication technologies (for example, direct one- and two-way coded communication via computer and phone lines), traditional communication through letter boxes has not lost its appeal. That channel is not as fast as electronic ones, but it is much safer. Even though counter-intelligence uses the newest methods to find hidden messages in the flow of posted correspondence, it is not that easy to reveal the presence of secret writing, not to mention the development of it.

During my time in Department 12, we also paid attention to the enormous possibilities presented by the international Human Genome Project for the Western counter-intelligence services.

Given samples against which to match, modern molecular biology techniques are able to identify any person, with an error-level approaching zero. In order to track accurately the identity of a living or a dead person, all that is required is a tiny amount of their biological material, for example a piece of hair, skin cells, drops of sweat or saliva, blood samples, even a particle of exhaled breath. By using such samples a modern laboratory can establish a genetic portrait of a person, an individual DNA profile.

Genetic information in the form of DNA maps, or individual DNA profiles, is collected in DNA databases. From the end of the 1990s, such DNA databases were being actively created in many developed countries. At first the reason was for research and medical purposes. But DNA profiles are analogous to fingerprints and they can be used as instruments to hunt down criminals. Modern forensic molecular techniques allow the identification of suspects or victims through the matching of DNA extracted from crime-scene samples virtually without mistake. Individual DNA profiles belonging to suspects of committed crimes, which are collected by the police, are compiled in national forensic DNA databases, which hold the profiles of all prisoners, offenders and suspected persons. From my perspective, the best forensic DNA database system exists in Scotland Yard, in England, which started to create national DNA crime databases and use DNA analysis right at the start of the 1990s. Next in order after England are the USA, the countries of Western Europe, Australia, New Zealand and the aggressive young biotechnological tigers of Eastern and Western Asia, including Singapore, Thailand and Malaysia, all of which have very recently joined the forensic DNA club.

All those whose DNA gets into these databases remain there; the information gathered in these forensic DNA databases is not destroyed, even after an individual's death. It is kept 'just in case' the police need to reinvestigate earlier crimes. During the last several years, national DNA systems have begun to be joined into a single united, international forensic DNA databank, the creation of which is a question of only a few years' additional progress away. In parallel with the creation of national forensic DNA systems developed by police and departments of internal affairs, DNA databases for missing persons and disaster-victim identification are also being created.

However, fighting crime, the search for missing persons and the identification of disaster victims are only the visible sides of the die. Another, hidden from the general public, is a lot more serious. The use of secret individual DNA profiles and national DNA databases is likely to have already been applied by most counter-intelligence services, first and foremost because they can provide more effective passport control at the border and make the search for this or that person a lot easier.

Individual DNA profiles can be created in secret – for example, during a physician's routine examination of a newborn and, at the same time, its mother; while undergoing examination by a general practitioner or the family doctor; during routine pregnancy examinations; while donating blood; during induction physicals for national service in the army, navy or air force; while taking drug tests during sporting events; during tests by traffic police for alcohol and drug usage, etc. The reader can easily lengthen this list.

I don't exclude the possibility that in some developed Western countries individual DNA profiles of their citizens are already going straight into secret databases. In any case, Russian counter-intelligence is unlikely to have missed this opportunity.

In this way, Western society becomes more and more transparent 'genetically', from the point of view of the police and counter-intelligence. But the same cannot be said about countries of the third world. The latter either don't yet have national individual DNA databases or their individual genetic profile systems are in the beginning stages and are unlikely to be brought on line in the near future. At the moment DNA profiling is still quite an expensive tool, one which only a few countries can allow themselves. But if a country doesn't have an effective system of personal identification – and at present there are both effective electronic fingerprint systems and national databases with DNA profiles – that means the third-world country will be under special scrutiny by Directorate S because it will be an easier country for Illegal Intelligence to use in order to document, deploy and plant Illegals. It is safer to carry out personal meetings with valuable secret agents in such countries; it is safer to infiltrate new Illegals to the West through them, or to recall to the Moscow Centre those who are under threat; and it is easier for an Illegal terrorist to escape through them after carrying out a special operation in a target country.

At the start of the 1990s we recommended to Departments 2 and 3 (i.e. of documentation and training of Illegals), and also to our colleagues from the 'diversionary and terrorism' Department 8, to start looking for ways to take advantage of the new 'opportunities' developing in the West. Department 2 had to search out professionals abroad who had access to individual DNA profiles, including the profiles of those who were dead.

With the help of such agents, it would be enough to obtain sets of genes of dead persons and apply them for the use of the future Illegals, or to enter the individual DNA profiles of Illegals into national DNA systems; and then it would be practically impossible for Western counter-intelligence to catch our people. The cover documentation of Illegals can be well-established by masquerading them or their presumed 'close relatives' as individuals who were born in those third-world countries that lacked sophisticated national identity databases. And the deployment to the West of our 'biological' Illegals – Illegalls who are terrorists, etc. – will be much safer through countries where passport control at the border does not use individual genetic-make-up profiles.

At the start of the 1990s, Department 3 had about ten Illegals, at various training stages, who were to work for Department 12. There were also five Illegals who had already gone through preliminary overseas training assignments and who were preparing for long-term settlement in the West. All those Illegals, apart from traditional intelligence and operational trainers, were specialists in various biological and medical areas. By the latter half of the 1990s they were to have been successfully legalised, settled and planted in host communities to start active work in their target countries. Add to them the already active Illegals of Department 12, then drag in the Illegals of the former Department 8…

It is hard to imagine how much effort, time and money are needed to train, place and settle successfully just one Illegal overseas. Training alone normally takes five to seven years: learning at least two foreign languages, one of which is polished to perfection as the Illegal's mother tongue; operational and intelligence training; learning precise details of the country where the Illegal is to live and work; and many other things. Typically, only a few individuals from among the hundreds selected by Department 3 successfully finished their training.

At some point in the late 1980s we calculated the cost of the several years of preselection, selection, checking out and training of one candidate, including the preparation of his or her bogus cover story and documentation. At that time the cost was equivalent to about US $200,000. At today's rates that could be the equivalent of $300,000–$400,000. Also to that must be added the expense of the 'running in' stage of the Illegal's deployment – his or her training missions to foreign countries – and his or her final dispatch or deployment to the target country. There were also operational costs incurred by the Line N Illegal Support officers of Directorate S in the Foreign Intelligence Service residences attached to the embassies to support the Illegal. Ah, yes, and there was the Illegal's salary.

Chapter 7

New Strategy

In times of peace, prepare for war
CHINESE PROVERB

C hanges in the Service began straight after Mikhail Gorbachev's rise to power. At the start, he astonished those of us in the Forest with his bravery. I remember with how much interest, we – the officers of Departments 8 and 12 (then just neighbours on the nineteenth floor) – regularly watched the television which was brought to us just for this event from the office of Brigadier Vladimir Kostikov, the head of Department 8. Putting immediate work aside, we glued ourselves to the TV, watching the first ever televised meetings of the Supreme Soviet of the USSR, where Gorbachev promised fast, radical changes in the country! Instead of the BBC, Deutsche Welle or Paris France, which we normally listened to in order to perfect our language skills, our personal short-wave radio receivers were tuned to Moscow programmes.

Nearly every morning our departmental meetings started off with discussions of the latest news – including what was said about us, about the Service, e.g. 'Are they really going to get rid of us?' A much-publicised move was started to declassify the KGB archives. Later, KGB Chairman Vadim Bakatin disclosed to the Americans the details of the electronic eavesdropping apparatus in the new US Embassy building in Moscow – a big gesture signalling 'friendship and trust'. It is unlikely that the Americans were taken in by this. But the effect of such events in Moscow on our espionage activities was something we had not counted on.

Our Illegals became agitated. At one operational meeting during this 'revolutionary' period of *perestroika*, Drozdov told us in confidence about the problems, which by then were evident even to him. He had started to receive personal letters from the Illegals. I was shocked that, breaking all our strict rules, Illegals went straight to the head of the Illegal Intelligence directorate. For an Illegal to approach the head of Directorate S could only mean one thing – something extraordinary had taken place.

'Personal letters are being written to me,' Drozdov admitted. 'They ask what is happening in our motherland. They say they can't understand anything! They ask who it is they are working for. Is it for the Soviet Union or for Russia? For the Communists or for the "new democrats"?'

It seemed that even Drozdov was unsure for whom they were working. Then he said, 'Our Illegals are very scared that the "democrats" in the government will betray them. And they write to me that, until order is restored in our country, they will not be maintaining contacts; it is for their own safety. They say that they will continue the long-term missions but will abstain from their next scheduled communications with the centre.'

And he joked gloomily, 'I have received not just one letter like this but several. What have they been doing? Have they held their own Party congress and started their own *coup d'état*?'

It was very strange for us to see the Illegals acting independently; in the past they had been wholly dependent on us. But it wasn't just confusion and fear that motivated them. They were concerned about the possibility that Moscow would abandon them, so if they had to get out of the countries where they were based they would have to do so on their own.

Naturally, this uncontrolled development of events in the country, which could have led to a diminishing of the role of our Service, troubled its leadership. Consequently the heads of the Foreign Intelligence Service were active members of the August 1991 anti-Gorbachev putsch which, in reality, had been planned for December 1990.

During the first hours of the August 1991 putsch, the confident, energetic General Drozdov had a sparkle in his eye as we stood in the duty-officer's room in Directorate S. From the windows of our headquarters in Yasenevo, we could see tanks moving towards Moscow's city centre along the ring road. When one of the officers present asked 'What will happen now?' Drozdov answered, 'We'll restore order in the country! We'll clear up the mess! It is about time!'

Then he added, 'We'd planned to push Gorbachev aside in December of last year, but cancelled at the last moment. We decided to wait. We thought that we could smarten up this crank in the Kremlin!'

I was very surprised to see General Drozdov in Directorate S that day because he'd already retired.

In the autumn of 1990, the centre's top leaders had decided to check their officers' loyalty. They wanted to see how the personnel would react in the case of armed revolt. They could come up with no better method than to create an imaginary attack on the Forest, alleging that crowds of pro-testers led by delegate-democrat Sergei Stankevich intended to attack us. Why Stankevich? Because he was most suitable to play the role of a 'sub-verting revolutionary': Popular, active, young, with good prospects – many saw him as Gorbachev's successor, especially after a photo of them together appeared in many newspapers around the world. And – icing on the cake – Stankevich lived in Yasenevo! And it was alleged that the unarmed fighters for 'freedom and democracy without the KGB' would attack our fortress right there in the Moscow suburb of Yasenevo! It was also alleged that they planned 'to capture the operational files and the KGB archives'.

Then began incredible turmoil! The whole centre was brought into action! We received weapons – pistols and even machine guns, which were kept in the multilevel basement of the central administration building – and were ordered to remain in our offices. It was an unusual sight for a peace-ful day – a big assembly of armed men, dressed in elegant suits. The entrances to the centre were blocked by fire-trucks with massive water cannon. We were drilled in repelling attackers! We lined up in living chains of officers. Through loudspeakers Party bigwigs explained how, having organised a live barricade, we were to retreat slowly behind the walls of the centre, and by doing that persuade the attacking rioters to disperse and go home! But, if the demonstrators did manage to burst through our barri-cades, we were to shelter behind the centre's fence, entering it through the only admission checkpoint in that part of the fence, one with narrow iron gates. The fire-trucks with massive water cannon would also be put into action – here there were no more than two or three. I asked myself what kind of panic and crush would take place at those gates; and how did they intend to determine, while in fire-trucks, who among the fugitives was backing off and who was attacking? Who was 'theirs', and who was 'ours'? Because we were not wearing Nevzorov's armbands.* If the protestors broke through our defences, that is, past our 'living chains', a three-metre wall, electrified barbed wire and a special armed Border Guard regiment, and appeared in the corridors of the interior buildings, we were ordered to defend the offices and safes with our Makarov pistols in our hands, that is, to shoot into crowds of unarmed, untrained people. But I asked myself what kind of a suicidal maniac would attempt to penetrate into those corridors? How many fanatics would be shot dead before the gates while those remaining, not frightened of pistol fire, managed to reach the safes?

It looked to me as if the scenario for our response to a 'planned attack' had been worked out in a hurry. Despite the obvious silliness of it all, many officers believed in the possibility of assault! Even so, the majority of us didn't intend to shoot Stankevich's supporters if it came to that.

'Severe' Stankevich and his 'gang of assistants' never did attack us. After day two, the fire-trucks disappeared from the gates of the central check-in point. But, by playing the Stankevich card, the conspirators did have an opportunity to see how the Service would behave itself if real revolutionary events began. Clearly, our leaders were able to convince themselves that there was no evidence of 'counter-revolutionaries' inside the Forest. So the mechanism to overthrow Gorbachev was put into action. But evidently because of that game play, the officers of the SVR became divided into two camps: 'Conservatives' and 'Democrats'. The latter were supporters of revolutionary change in our society. The Conservatives acted confident and were very self-assured. They bravely criticised Gorbachev, his group of economists and reformers, and those within the Service who were known to be aligned to their point of view. Democrats decided to vote by leaving through the open door. The younger, active and democratically minded

* Alexander Nevzorov, a St Petersburg journalist known for his provocative TV programmes on the eve of the August 1991 *coup d'état*. On one of his programmes the government's supporters – an elite group of KGB Spetsnaz (the equivalent of the British SAS) – wore armbands with the word 'ours'.

officers retired. They were about one third of the centre's personnel. Most of them now work in well-known Russian banks, firms and joint ventures, or are representatives of foreign companies selling Russian metal, oil, diamonds and military technology.

After the fall of the Soviet Union, many officers from former Soviet republics – e.g. the Balts, the Armenians, the Georgians, the Kazakhs – moved to their ethnic homelands to work in their national secret intelligence services, many of which would operate against Russia and would not be allies of the Russian Foreign Intelligence Service. Their leaving was a big loss for Russian state security and its Intelligence Service, because those officers knew the Service perfectly from the inside – its strategy, tactics, methods, spy-rings and strictly guarded state secrets. Some of my former colleagues attained new heights in their ethnic homelands. For example, Lieutenant Colonel A. became one of the Kirghiz president's personal advisers; while Major A. is now an ambassador of Uzbekistan in South-East Asia.

They say that nobody leaves the Intelligence Service, even after they resign. My colleague Captain Andrei F—ov left Department 12 a year after me. Officially he resigned from the Service, but he remained working in the German pharmaceutical firm G., one of the commercial covers of Department 12. He actively helped the department: he made profitable commercial contacts with pharmaceutical firms, opened bank accounts, created branches of the cover firm in Western Europe, and even kept up communication with the director of the company, Mr Rainer B. (who was a long-standing agent of Department 12). Andrei told me, 'They need me! I can freely travel to Europe, make deals, make money for them. And they allow me to make money, and they also protect me. This kind of alliance works for me.'

'They need you now,' I said, 'when you carry hot coals from the fire for them. When they settle in, and their people will be able to do what you do, they will get rid of you.' This was likely to be the truth.

Alongside Andrei was another officer of Department 12, Major Valery K. In our European Section he'd been no genius but he served with sweat and blood, and he drudged from one rank to another. He did not run valuable agents and Illegals, and never initiated anything. In the cover firm G. he was suitable neither for operational nor for commercial work. But he remained in the firm to look after Andrei. Andrei had to accept the situation. I am told that the cover firm G. still exists. However, its Moscow division is a company officially affiliated with the philanthropic (!) organisation 'Veterans of the Russian Foreign Intelligence Service', which was created in 1993 by the former head of the Service, General Leonid Shebarshin.

Major Dmitry V., my colleague in Directorate S, got a job in a foreign bank's Moscow branch. Another friend – Major Nikolai G., the officer from Directorate K (External Counter-Intelligence) – is now a director of a large Russian firm which sells metal overseas. Captain Yuri S. works in an insurance company and represents the interests of the De Beers diamond company on the Russian market. Those officers continued to keep in touch with the Service even after their official resignations. And the Service helps them. I know of many similar examples.

I am very confident that most of the prominent Russian banks, joint ventures, and commercial firms were (and I believe continue to be) under the strict control and unwavering surveillance of the Russian secret services. The secret war between Russian financial institutions and big companies in order to increase profits and, as a consequence, increase their influence and power in the country, has been carried out, in reality, mainly between Russia's secret services. Serious analysis of Russia's current economic state and the true reasons why government reforms are or are not being implemented would require, first of all, that one discover which service's interests the reforms affect.

Even though the 1991 putsch failed, it nevertheless accelerated dramatic changes in the Russian Foreign Intelligence Service. The Service was depoliticised, and at the same time the operationally worthless – what we sometimes called 'ballast' – was got rid off. Officers of pensionable age were sent off to retirement, and many auxiliary and administrative structures with unjustifiably inflated staff levels were reduced or abolished.

Part of the remaining intelligence establishment was quietly moved under new 'commercial' cover but remained working in the Service. By taking that step the Foreign Intelligence Service widened the sphere of its control and influence inside Russia as well as in target countries. In the latter, commercial cover gave its officers the opportunity for wider and deeper access to banks, companies, firms, etc. And inside Russia it broadened its access and influence through placing its people in vital posts within the economy and the government. The Russian intelligence community worked to make progress for itself, installing its people into the new economic structures and political organisations. That way it could take advantage of developing situations within the country. It is easiest to do that if one controls both the financial resources and the strategic raw materials; who controls them controls the country.

The Russian Foreign Intelligence Service reformed, but it did not weaken. With the influx of several more young officers having the highest medical, biological and agricultural qualifications, Department 12 even gained strength. Most of the new officers were enlisted into the American Section, the 'line' that flourished most after the Service was reformed. Clearly the USA still remained a major espionage target. In fact it was even more important than before. Department 12 was also strengthened with experienced officers from other departments of Directorate S and Directorate T. Nearly all of them were transferred to us from Department 4, which operated against the USA on the American continent. They were appointed to Department 12 straight after finishing their tours of duty in the USA and the Columbian *rezidenturas*. Of course, we continued to help train and dispatch new Illegals and to recruit secret agents, and the flow of biological materials received through the VOLNA channel was also growing. Overseas assignments of our officers into the Russian Foreign Intelligence Service *rezidenturas* in the countries of the 'main enemy', i.e. the countries of NATO and the USA, also continued. For example, half of my colleagues from the European Section operated as Line N Illegal Support officers in the Vienna and Bonn residencies.

Even at the beginning of the 1990s – a period of 'warming' relationships with the West – Directorate S never took this new relationship to heart. Even during the period of so-called 'détente', Illegal Intelligence continued to follow the invariable principle of espionage – 'espionage works best and is most successful during periods of peace'. For us that meant: while favourable circumstances exist it is essential to utilise the respite to deploy to the West as many Illegals as possible and to cultivate and recruit more special agents.

Since our 'Door to the West' – the Directorate S *rezidentura* in East Berlin, which our department used to launch Illegals into the West – was soon to be shut down, we tried to use it as often as we could. From 1990 to 1992, the East Berlin *rezidentura*, together with its local stations in almost every big city of East Germany (e.g. Dresden, Leipzig), was actively used by Department 12. In East Berlin we had operational apartments with numerous servicing staff. In these our officers met and worked with Illegals and valuable agents who had been clandestinely transported from West to East Berlin. In East Berlin, Department 12 possessed external secret surveillance which could also operate in West Berlin. East Berlin was also used for communication with important agents who operated in Western Europe.

The 'reforms' I mentioned earlier extended to Department 12 as well; another line of work was activated, the commercial one. Using our agent networks and informal contacts among overseas businessmen, about a quarter of the officers were deployed under cover in Western firms and joint ventures. Business cover provided better security for our operations in target countries. For example, based on a Drozdov order, Department 12 did not inform embassy *rezidenturas* in target countries that our officers were also operating there under commercial cover. Another important advantage of the new cover positions was the opportunity they provided for officers to travel more freely within target countries. Such movement is very plausibly masqueraded as a 'business necessity' and it increases the opportunity to communicate with deep-cover agents. That kind of freedom of action is not possible when one is working under diplomatic cover from one of the Russian embassies. Another advantage was the much wider possibility of establishing prospective contacts with people who are 'objectives' of Department 12. Commercial cover gave us the ability to self-fund some operations. Traditional espionage activity requires significant funding, which has to be handled very carefully. It is obvious that to use Russian bank accounts openly to hand over money to an Illegal or to a secret agent is impossible. That would easily be spotted by the enemy's counter-intelligence. So money has to pass along a difficult and complicated route in order to cleanse it of the tiniest Russian stain before it can be given to an agent. Commercial cover allowed Department 12 to carry out operations in the West without having to be so devious.

The weak side of using commercial cover is the lack of protection of the kind that diplomatic status confers. The absence of such status requires that the intelligence officer take very great care; the smallest error could result in his arrest.

One of the first positive commercial experiences of Department 12 was a joint-venture company which we codenamed CITADEL. At the end of 1989 I sent a report to General Drozdov in which I explained the advantages and new possibilities of using commercial cover in the interests of Department 12, and I proposed that we use CITADEL. Drozdov agreed to the proposal and soon permission for the operation was received from the Service's head, Lieutenant General Leonid Shebarshin.

CITADEL was organised under Department 12's control and had its own branches in Russia, Western and Eastern Europe, and affiliated companies in South-East Asia, including Singapore and Hong Kong. Among its first major commercial deals was the selling of Russian crude oil, which straight away brought millions of US dollars' profit. The president of the firm was my agent codenamed GRIN.

About a year later, using the opportunities provided by CITADEL and the support of GRIN, I was able to prepare new independent cover positions in West Germany, Hungary and England. I made several trips to Budapest and Frankfurt-am-Main. We were able to prove quickly to Drozdov the effectiveness of also using CITADEL as a means of cultivating prospective agents and making recruitment approaches to biology researchers. For example, in West Germany, while buying new antiviral vaccines against infections of fish for a commercial trout farm in Russia, we were able to establish informal relations with an employee of one of the big biotechnological research companies in West Germany. In another case, by patenting in Hungary and in West Germany technical procedures facilitating the detection of biological toxins and chemical agents, including nerve gases, I was able to gain access to confidential information of biotech company T. in Frankfurt-am-Main. Using my position in CITADEL, I began to cultivate two key specialists, one from T. itself and another from its affiliated firm W. in Birmingham, England.

In CITADEL I became responsible for locating the most commercially effective technologies and their marketing and sale on the Western market. Part of the profit from the sale of these new technologies was set aside for my new group. By putting it to use, Department 12 could provide financial independence to this cover position and create new ones, as well as support its Illegals and agents.

The idea of using new technologies, especially those which could be used in biotechnology, attracted us in Department 12 because they would make possible unsuspected approaches to our objectives in target countries.

The first successfully marketed technology we had was developed by two secret research centres controlled by the KGB. They were involved in a top-secret programme to develop and modernise chemical and toxin warfare. A version of the new technology had already been put to use by the Ministry of Defence to detect even the smallest leaks from submarine hulls, atomic power plants, intercontinental ballistic missiles with nuclear warheads, aircraft fuel tanks, and secret laboratories where chemical and biological weapons were being produced. Since the middle of the 1980s, counter-intelligence had also used it effectively to find secret writing in the stream of correspondence into and out of the country through the Central Post Office in Moscow.

An advertisement about the new technology, which I put into one quite well-known Hungarian commercial journal, soon spread across European countries and interested many Western commercial firms.

Using CITADEL as a cover, I also had an opportunity to get access to some of our department's objectives in Iran and Israel. These were contacts who were interested in buying new systems for the early detection of chemical and biological weapons.

I had to use CITADEL for clandestine work with some of our Illegals and special agents who operated in Europe: first of all with ANVAR, who had successfully resumed work in the Scandinavian countries a year before; and, if necessary, to help to support ROSA. These were my prime secret tasks in CITADEL.

Successful use of the CITADEL cover enabled Department 12 to establish and use other commercial masquerades in a short space of time. In Department 12's European Section we actively made use of the West German commercial pharmaceutical firm G. and joint Russian–French enterprise S., which traded medicine and medical technologies. Straight away three officers of our European Section started to use these covers. Among the clients of firm G. were private medical clinics, pharmacological and biotechnological companies, research laboratories and medical centres in various West European countries, which made human and animal hormones, drugs, vaccines and cultures of novel genetically altered micro-organisms. The director of this private company – agent Rainer B. – helped us to open a number of accounts under false names in banks in Monaco, Liechtenstein, France and Germany. Simultaneous with the creation of the cover G., Department 12 also gained an independent channel which delivered biological and pharmacological agents. This channel was auxiliary to the main VOLNA channel. Samples of new biomaterials and medicines obtained by our agents were delivered to Moscow as if they were normal medicines from Germany. Among the customs officials on the border were 'our people', i.e. support agents.

The moment which I consider to be the most vital in the growth of Department 12 was its consolidation in 1992 with the officially disbanded Department 8. Among the main tasks of Department 8 were the training of deep-cover agents, Illegal terrorists and fighters responsible for the preparation and carrying out of single and massive terrorist acts, acts of sabotage and diversion, and the clandestine murder of troublemakers in target countries. The main targets of Department 8 on the territory of an assumed enemy were both military and civil. Department 8's people were also trained to assassinate government officials in important positions in various target countries in the event of a large-scale war or a local military conflict.

Over a number of years, Department 8 had established secret training camps in many of the world's hot spots. It also had training bases in the Crimea, in the North Caucasus, in the 'social democracies' and other countries amicably disposed towards the USSR in Africa, Indo-China, Asia and Latin America. I was aware of overseas training bases in Cuba, Vietnam and Mozambique. Apart from the 'usual suspects' listed above, Department 8 actively operated in West Germany, Britain and Australia. Its officers were always away on covert missions and most actively operated in the troubled areas of the planet. More often than any other officers in Directorate S, officers of Department 8 were awarded combat orders and medals in peace time. Selection, recruitment, training and preparation of Department 8's secret supporters continued unceasingly abroad.

Department 8 taught its trainee professionals to fire practically every kind of small arm in the world.

The arsenal of special resources available to Department 8 was extensive, ranging from 'quiet' methods of killing, for example quick-acting poisons, to 'louder' ones, including a diverse range of explosives. One example was so-called 'deadly water', with which I was acquainted while visiting a terrorist training centre located near the town of Balashikha in the Moscow region. This 'deadly water' was a liquid explosive of great destructive power. It had no colour or odour. It could have been poured into a glass as an ordinary drink, into a fountain pen instead of ink, hidden at the bottom of a bottle or decanter. It could also be hidden, say, under the coller of the victim's jacket or overcoat. It could easily be detonated at a distance via a radio signal. A man's jacket impregnanted with the explosive was hung over a metal pole the size of a man. It worked marvellously! How inventive man is at killing his own kind!

The training camp in Cuba was used from 1990 to 1991 especially intensively (it was shut down in 2003). This was not long before Department 8 was absorbed into Department 12. At that time, the number of assignments of Department 8's officers to countries of the Far East and the Pacific rim countries also grew. The head of Department 8, Brigadier Vladimir Kostikov, and his officers visited Cuba more than any other country during that period and spent weeks at a time there. During those years massive diseases of domestic pig stocks were observed in Cuba, and I assume that the visits were somehow connected with these atypical outbreaks.

Department 8 always had great autonomy within Directorate S. Apart from a secret direct phone line between the KGB station in Cuba and Department 8 (to the communication room next door to Brigadier Kostikov's office), there was also a direct phone line between Department 8 and all the overseas KGB residencies. The brigadier was in the habit of calling his department out of the blue from any country of the world where he happened to be and straight away giving orders to his subordinates or delivering yet another dressing down. It was not known why the severe Brigadier Kostikov often ignored the other secure channel, i.e. why he did not use coded cables. Did he feel independent? Did he want to avoid control by Drozdov? If so, then why did Kostikov feel in need of provoking confrontation? Perhaps the freedom-loving and independent brigadier deliberately sought it? Believed that he was indispensable to the Service and thought he might succeed Drozdov as chief of Illegal Intelligence?

Famous veterans of clandestine terrorism worked in Department 8. Two of them had earned the 'Hero of the Soviet Union' and the 'Order of

Lenin' medals – the highest awards in the Soviet Union. One of them, Colonel Yuzbashyan, was well known for troop-train derailments behind German lines during World War II. Short, always smiling, dressed in a baggy suit, he did not look like a mad warrior intent on taking out troop trains. Yuzbashyan operated no less actively after the war, transferring his experience and skills to his colleagues, Illegals and special agents who went on to complete assignments in many countries. Yuzbashyan left Directorate S and, in 1992, accepted the post of Chairman of the KGB of the newly independent state of Armenia. Soon afterwards he was shot dead near his home in Erevan, the capital. His wife, who might otherwise have suffered the same fate, hid in Moscow with close relatives who were friends of my family.

The close partnership of Department 12 and Department 8 began some years before they were joined. At the start there were periodic joint Party and operational meetings. In due time we came to have a closer partnership. Initially that started with our advising officers of Department 8 in the fields of biological and medical sciences. Then we were requested to advise them of vulnerable targets on foreign territory, the kind of targets the destruction of which – or even short-term disruption of which – could have severe ecological, agricultural and public-health consequences. Soon after that, we started to receive requests from Department 8 for more detailed descriptions of the defining distinctive features of our kind of objective – targets such as biological and medical research laboratories and centres, biological and pharmacological companies, etc., in which experiments with potential pathogenic micro-organisms and bacteria of deadly diseases of humans, animals and plants might have been carried out. I also had to participate in that work. I received orders straight form the head of Department 12 that I get acquainted with routine secret operational documents received from Department 8. In most cases I was asked to carry out analysis of the suitability and effectiveness of the places selected for the potential clandestine storage of containers with dangerous biological materials and toxins so that when needed – i.e. on 'D-Day' – they could be used to disable or destroy the objectives.

I remember well one of the operational files given to me for analysis and recommendation. Five pages of typed text with attached diagrams and clandestine photos of places selected for dead drops close to a naval base in Australia, which was used by ships of the US Navy. I had to evaluate whether the places selected were suitable for infecting or poisoning the naval garrison through, for example, a local water supply system, or by using transport entering the base, or through the dispersal of spores of dangerous bacteria near air-conditioning and ventilation systems. My assessment and recommendation was needed for one of the deep-cover agents of Department 8 in Australia.

With the absorption of the old Department 8, the reorganised and expanded 'biological' department became the biggest operational department of Directorate S, nearly doubling the number of its officers once again. After the unification the targets and assignments of the two formerly independent departments were combined and the new Department 12 concentrated more on combat tasks. It also received a new designation, '8'. The head of the newly established Department 8 remained Colonel Leonid Bouz.

Our relationships with Department 1 – the Special Reserve of Directorate S – also became more active. The Special Reserve was one of the most highly compartmented groups in Illegal Intelligence. The officers of Department 1 were mostly former Illegals themselves who, after long years of active work overseas under assumed names and cover stories, had returned to the centre. They carried out the most dangerous and risky operations, which might last from a few weeks to several months or a year. Their missions were particularly important tasks ordered by the chiefs of the Service and the highest authority of the country. Such tasks might include the 'false-flag' recruitment as an agent of our Service a foreign citizen who would believe he was working for someone else, a real or invented organisation, or even a non-Russian secret intelligence service. This would be necessary, say, when dealing with an Illegal working under conditions which preclude all contact with the local Russian Foreign Intelligence Service legal *rezidentura*, or in the absence of a *rezidentura* in the target country or in the country where the Illegal operates. Few in Directorate S knew all the operations and assignments of Department 1. But it has to be stated that – having very reliable cover documents (genuine passports and other identification); native fluency in a foreign language; cover stories with well-supported 'real' facts; and not once having been under suspicion by foreign counter-intelligence services – these professionals are able to carry out even the toughest clandestine combat operations. So, for example, at one of the department's operational meetings Colonel Bouz passed comment on the potential use of the Special Reserve's Illegals in the interests of Department 12, i.e. to carry out acts of biological sabotage and terrorism in the event of war. Knowing quite well how close and unofficial relationships were between Colonel Bouz and the head of Directorate S, General Drozdov, I do not exclude that the option had been discussed by them beforehand. Even our colleagues from Department 8 had hinted about their special official relationships with Illegals from the Special Reserve group.

One of the most deeply concealed 'business' operations of our department was the trade in precious stones on the Western European black market. The secrecy of the operation was of the highest order. Only three persons at the Centre were involved in the details: the head of Directorate S, General Drozdov, who personally controlled the operation; the head of Department 12, Colonel Bouz, who organised the deal; and I, a captain, whose CITADEL operation was used to sell the precious stones. Colonel Bouz thought that my operational cover in CITADEL and its office in Budapest were perfect for that purpose. The goal of the operations, I thought, was good – to get more secure financial support for our agents and Illegals. It seemed to me that this new plan, which was approved by General Drozdov, would help to support the department's main tasks and operations. Oh to be young and naïve!

Neither our agent in Latin America, from whom the emeralds got to our officer Colonel Vladimir Y., who worked under cover in Columbia, nor agent GRIN, who sold the emeralds in Europe, knew all the details; they were only responsible for their parts of the deal. My head, Colonel Bouz, took great care that the details of my work under the cover of CITADEL were closed off from him – the agents and contacts drawing Drozdov into this and similar operations were too deeply planted and valuable. Addressed to Colonel Bouz, the emeralds arrived in a sealed container at the centre via the VOLNA channel. He personally went to the Moscow international airport, Sheremetevo-2, to receive the containers with the precious stones.

Not long before we sold the first emeralds, GRIN and I were sitting in a bar in the old city of Buda – a chic region of Budapest. GRIN asked me, 'Do I have to become more sensitive to danger once I start this business? Can you guarantee my safety?'

'As long as you are with us,' I answered, 'you don't have to be afraid of anything. But we have to follow your every step, your every action so that we can solve any problems that might pop up.'

GRIN did not follow my advice. After two successful years of trading, he decided to carry through one of the deals without our surveillance. He went into debt then went bankrupt and finally went on the run.

The task of paying agents and financially supporting Illegals was always a hard job for Directorate S, and it was the same within our department. The main aim of the black-market operations was to eliminate the smallest sign that the money belonged to organisations which were connected to Russia. Experience showed that Department 12's new commercial covers were an excellent way of laundering money for our people abroad.

At the order of Colonel Bouz, I organised a personal meeting for him with agent GRIN. I had to prepare the agent to understand that he would benefit from our regularly supplying precious stones for the deals. Each lot was to sell for US $50,000–$100,000. I saw that GRIN wasn't really into this 'Russian business', but, dependent on us, he had no way out.

The first emeralds were delivered to Budapest by Colonel Bouz. In order to avoid customs examining his personal belongings and causing any unnecessary publicity, he flew using a diplomatic passport and an assumed name. The first stock was worth a relatively small amount – about $40,000.

Bouz persuaded the agent, whom I had prepared for the possibility of serious business, easily. GRIN was invited to celebrate at a five-star restaurant situated in the middle of an artificial lake in the old city, in Pest. The prospects seemed excellent.

After the first stock of emeralds was sold to black-market dealers in Western Europe, I came to understand that the operations were being carried out very much in the personal interests of my bosses: the biggest part of the profit that came from the sale of the stones was going directly into their pockets. When my bosses planned to utilise the CITADEL cover and the VOLNA channel for the purpose of selling Russian diamonds in the West, I started to become anxious, fearing that the department's tasks, which I had to carry out in Western Europe using CITADEL cover, could be threatened with disruption or complete failure. It was terribly wrong to mix the clandestine operations of Directorate S with the pursuit of personal enrichment. That was what pushed me to think about leaving the Forest.

On the outside, it would have seemed that everything was going along nicely for me. I was in line for rapid career advancement – today or tomorrow I would be sent to England for a long-term assignment, promoted to the military rank of major, and could expect special attention from the department's head and even the attention of the leader of Directorate S. What more could I have wished for? Then, soon after the successful sale of the first stock of emeralds, my boss called me into his office and offered me several printed certificates recording shares of stock in the MiG and Sukhoi companies, the world-famous military aircraft manufacturers. 'We trust you,' he said. 'Here are some shares, part of an exclusive offer – take a dozen.' He put down in front of me onto the table a large envelope which he'd taken out of his safe. 'Only a few people in our Directorate are being offered these shares.' Then he added, 'Big prospects are opening up for you. You only need to behave right.'

Was I being threatened, or was he only offering sound advice? To this day I thank God that I refused the shares and did not become a hostage to them.

After that, work in the Intelligence Service became a burden. I told my wife that I planned to leave not only the department but the Russian Foreign Intelligence Service altogether. At that time she was working for one of the popular national newspapers. She was scared and anxious about my leaving a well-paid job with excellent prospects to go 'nowhere'. But she approved of my decision. Like me, she cherished independence. She said, 'I see. "Happy to serve, but not to be subservient"! '

In spring 1992 I submitted a letter of resignation to the department and the Service, in which I explained my decision. I said I thought it was impossible for me to continue working in the department, where personal pecuniary interests were endangering the work of Directorate S. A Directorate S Personnel Department officer then called me to his office to ask me to rewrite the letter, to say that 'I left to join the civil sector of the country's economy with the wish to use my scientific and professional knowledge for the good of society'. Clearly, I was not the first officer in the Service to take such a step, and it seemed to me that my letter was received quite calmly. However, Colonel Bouz did call me to his office for a 'heart-to-heart' talk, and he invited me to dine with him several times. He really did not want to part with me.

But a new life opened up before me. The life of an ordinary citizen, without the benefit of a large, powerful organisation on which to depend. Yet I never regretted it. I found work in Moscow as an assistant to a trade representative working for a Latin American country.

Who did I not encounter during my year at that job! Former policemen from England – mediators, who sold and hired Russian transport helicopters and mid-size passenger aircraft to Africa, Asia and Latin American countries. Former Soviet ambassadors and trade representatives in Central and Latin American countries. Former and serving officers in the field from the GRU and the SVR. Generals who'd served in Afghanistan and military prosecutors from the former Baltic republics and newly independent Central Asian states, who opened companies to trade stocks and military equipment that remained on the territories of the former Soviet republics. Directors of well-known Russian military and industrial corporations, quiet Serbians and Croatians, who cautiously made inquiries about arms for the independent republics of the former Yugoslavia. Russian ethnic Kurds, who wished to buy military uniforms for their Muslim brothers in the Near East. Businessmen from St Petersburg, who transferred large amounts of money from Russian banks to the West. Shabby merchants from Texas – sellers of old stock, who came to 'wild' Russia to chase easy money. A respectable Indonesian businessman, Dr H., with an official warrant from the Naval Ministry to find ways to buy small ships for coastal defence, high-speed shipboard and self-propelled rocket launchers...

My new workplace was located in an old, shabby house in Smolenka. There were a lot of negotiations, a lot of meetings, a lot of hopes. But there were few results. I soon realised that the 'private firm' for which I worked was not at all what it seemed. Its real aim was not buying and selling but the secret gathering of information about businessmen and political figures who wished to be involved in 'cool' businesses. The former KGB counter-intelligence service, the FSK, controlled the firm and its director Mr M. – a citizen of a Latin American country and a long-serving KGB agent – placing him in the role of informant. Mr M., former trade representative and diplomat, had worldwide connections.

Mr M. was in no hurry to return to his homeland in Latin America. While he was alone with me, he frequently brought up the infamous 'Colombian tie', which the drug mafia uses to settle scores with its own renegades: as a punishment for treason the informer's throat is cut and the trachea pulled out and placed on the chest like a tie. It was confusing to me. Was he afraid of his distant compatriots or of the Russian secret service?

Well, I was sick of the whole business. I knew I would have to move on if I was to retain my sense of integrity.

In 1993 my wife and I started to think about leaving our mother country. If it were not for dramatic changes in the country and the fall of the Soviet Union, I would have served with truth and honour for my motherland. My wife and I sincerely welcomed Gorbachev's and Yeltsin's reforms, believing in the necessity of change. But we could not accept what came with *perestroika* – the crime boom, bribery, corruption, the growing gap between rich and poor. People in our motherland were still not free politically or economically.

By this time an ever-increasing number of Russian people had started to leave the country: some as tourists, others for ever. For me, a former career intelligence officer who had at one time worked for one of the nation's most secret organisations, to leave the country permanently was practically impossible. As a former intelligence officer, I could have left Russia using a tourist or a business visa then sought political refugee status. I knew how to leave the country secretly because I had mastered a lot of 'trade craft', including exfiltration. But I did not wish to be a turncoat. So I had to use old and new contacts, knowledge and skills which I acquired during my years of work in the Service, and other connections I had because of my qualifications as a scientist. We were very lucky. It was difficult, but by taking advantage of some of the bureaucratic muddle that existed in Russia at that time we obtained visas to enable us to enter a new country. That happened towards the end of 1994.

It was very sad to leave our own mother country. Until the moment of our departure, we could not believe that we would be brave enough to take the step. My wife, especially, could not imagine how she would live in a foreign land without the Moscow theatres and galleries, without her friends and colleagues. Last, but not least, there were our families and relations. Neither of us could know if we would ever be able to see our loved ones again.

At the end of 1994, a day before our flight, we rapidly said goodbye to our Moscow – the Moscow we had come to love so much. One last time we walked along the lanes and boulevards where we'd spent our earlier years, where we knew nearly every bench by the Patriarchy ponds, every bend of the Spiridonievsky lane and the courtyards with lilacs on the Old Arbat.

Now, as we sat inside our plane, snow was beating obliquely against the windows, which made the lights on the runway of airport Sheremetevo-2 murky. The morning thaw and thick fog, unusual for December, had been replaced by a sudden frost and great blizzard. Then the time came for the Boeing's pilot to run up the plane's engines, while waiting for the control tower to give him clearance for take-off. It seemed to me then that the flight was being held for quite a while. I thought to myself, 'The airport says that it is because of the blizzard, but what if...?' Clearly, wild and crazy thoughts were circling around my head. 'What if the plane is being held back because of us? They'll arrive any minute and won't let us out of the country.'

How astonishing are such fears for a Westerner; how natural they are for any Russian who has ever left the country!

But everything turned out OK; soon, our plane lifted into the air.

Chapter 8

International Biological Security –
Is It Achievable?

migration is a drama to every Russian. For my wife and I it was
especially so. In Moscow we had belonged to a small privileged
group of people connected with the highest state secrets. We lived
in an isolated world and were preoccupied with our work. Our daughters
went to a special kindergarten for children whose fathers were KGB officers.
Our circle of contacts was limited to fellow KGB colleagues and their
families (plus a handful of close friends from my wife's theatre, artistic and
journalist circles – but contacts like those were generally not welcome).
Unauthorised contacts with foreigners, even from Eastern Bloc countries,
were out of the question. KGB families were consciously settled in the same
block of flats so that it would be easier for our counter-intelligence service
to eavesdrop on our telephone conversations, watch over our private lives,
and collect information about our close relatives.

After emigrating, we found ourselves one of the many families who come
to a foreign country in search of a happier life. Nobody could even imagine
our real background. My wife would sometimes say, 'Alexander, wouldn't it
be great if we had an ordinary past? Will we really always be unable to trust
people and not let them get close to us?'

I completed a few courses in a local university in the country we had
settled in, and in the evenings after lectures I worked. My first job was
low-paid manual labour and did not require any qualifications or any specific knowledge. Later I started work on a second PhD, one in international

environmental law. My wife also changed her profession. She was always a great piano player so in our new country she opened a music school, and she is often in demand as a freelance pianist.

I applied for many jobs and received more than one hundred letters of rejection before finally obtaining an interesting offer – working for the local city government, which led to a position in a government ministry: both jobs being in the area of environmental and public-health science.

Having been, so to speak, a poacher, I am now a gamekeeper. It seems unbelievable to me that I am working in an organisation in a Western country that my former Department 12 colleagues would regard as a worthy espionage target.

With great interest I continue to keep up with modern molecular/genetic-research developments. I also pay particular attention to risk assessments of these experiments and related issues of international law, and publish my own articles in this area. I find that in no country is there any mechanism for effective protection of people from biological and toxin weapons and from terrorist acts involving them. I think that my opinion would be shared by many officers of the intelligence services of leading countries, because they are involved in monitoring and trying to gauge the extent of biological espionage activities.

My past profession as a career Russian Foreign Intelligence Service officer, to which I gave almost ten years of my life, taught me to see things others probably do not notice. The inexplicable infections that affected wild and domestic stock as well as humans in China and Hong Kong in 1997, foot-and-mouth disease in England in 2001, a new virus infection (severe acute respiratory syndrome, or SARS) in China and Hong Kong that spread across nearly the whole world in 2003, two plague epidemics in Western India in September and October 1994, an epidemic of Congo-Crimea haemorrhagic fever in Oblivskaya village in the Rostov region in Russia in July 1999, West Nile fever in the Volgograd region in Russia, and non-specific outbreaks in some countries and regions over the last few years: I believe that many of these incidents are a likely result of secret biological research experiments or the accidental releases of new anti-crop and anti-livestock weapons into the open environment. Could it be that some of these 'case studies' – the outbreaks of which may imply the use of pathogens in their less dangerous forms – were carried out to test future potential wide-scale use of biological warfare?

The threat does not originate from just one part of the world. And neither are the potential effects of the threat restricted to just one part of the world. In 1989 Britain and the United States officially declared the termination of their own secret programmes of biological weapons development. In 1992* Russia joined them, officially declaring the termination of its secret germ-warfare programme. But let us not forget that accumulated scientific-research for biological weapons development in those countries did not disappear with the mothballing of their biological warfare programmes.

When, in December 1984, I was enlisted into Directorate S's Department 12, not all of its vacancies were yet occupied. About half of its then twenty offices on the nineteenth floor in the new building at the Yasenevo Headquarters were empty. At the time, there were fourteen officers of Department 12. In 1992, when I was about to leave the Foreign Intelligence Service, the 'biological' department had doubled in staff. It had increased even during the time of general staff reduction and the mass exodus of career Foreign Intelligence Service officers. Its doubling in size also coincided with the period of 'democratisation' of the Russian intelligence services and the warming of relationships with NATO and the USA. In a world that was seen to be moving toward détente, this did not seem to make sense. But it did indeed make sense. It meant that biological warfare programmes in Russia and, possibly, in other countries of the world, did not close down, but continued to grow. It suggests that governments' interest in biological weapons – silent, compact, cheap and difficult to detect – continued to expand with each passing day.

I believe that intelligence agencies of leading countries, including my former colleagues, continue to investigate secret experiments with biological warfare agents, steal biological secrets from each other, and procure new vaccines, modified strains of dangerous pathogens and cultures of offensive biological agents. It is hard to believe that, despite the official end of biological weapons programmes, countries which beforehand were developing them have stopped spying on each other.

Here and there, new facts demonstrate that various countries of the world continue research in this area. According to the German newspaper *Bild*, from the mid-1990s until the present secret research has continued in

* In 1992 Department 12 and Department 8 were joined.

Bundeswehr medical laboratories located in Munich, Bavaria and Münster, Low Saxony. By 2003, according to information from journalists, the overall mass of allocations for such investigations had grown by 30 per cent when compared with 1997. According to some Western intelligence agencies, Israel is working on a biological weapon which would harm Arabs but not Jews. In order to create such a weapon which is also called an 'ethnic', or a 'genetic', weapon, Israeli scientists would have to apply discoveries of genetics and medicine which identify genes possessed only by Arabs.

The biological institute Nes Tsiona, which is working to bring this programme to life, is assumed to be the main centre of Israeli research into chemical and biological weapons. Even though the task of creating an 'ethnic' weapon is quite difficult, as both Arabs and Jews have Semitic origins, Israeli scientists say that they have already succeeded in isolating specific traits of the unique genetic profiles of some ethnic Arab groups. These investigations are practically identical to those which were carried out by South African scientists in the apartheid period. Dr Daan Gusen, the head of the South African Centre of Chemical and Biological War, confirmed in 2003 that in the 1980s his group ordered investigation into the possibility of developing 'skin and colour weapons', aimed at people with black skin. According to information provided in *Jane's* magazine, which specialises in analysing problems of defence and security, Israel's scientists used South African researches in an attempt to create an 'ethnic' weapon that would be effective against Arabs.

In 1999 the Malaysian newspaper *Sun* said that the Malaysian cabinet suspected foreigners were using a deadly new virus spread by pigs to sabotage the local economy. The newly detected, previously unknown virus caused an epidemic, which affected Malaysia and Singapore in 1998 and 1999, killing more than 120 people. The Malaysian Health Ministry believed that it was difficult to ignore indications of a foreign link to the outbreak and suspected that it was likely to be a clandestine foreign operation to undermine the country's agriculture through biological warfare. Among other factors which raised that suspicion were the characteristics of the virus. This situation seems to parallel that of the outbreak of the SARS virus in 2003 and 2004.

On 2 August 2002, an epidemic of a strange influenza occurred in five of the six provinces of the island of Madagascar. Only in the province of

Antseranana, in the country's north-east, was not one case registered. There were about 23,000 cases of the disease, and 671 people died.

Doctors observed that those who became sick didn't last for more than two days; but what really alarmed the special medical UN team that went to Madagascar was that, in general, the epidemic only harmed the people of one ethnic group.

In 1993, in the Four Corners area of New Mexico in the USA, close to the US Army's Fort Wingate biowarfare testing area, a mysterious disease broke out which, initially, also seemed to be either a normal flu or some acute respiratory disease. But it seemed impossible to cure those who were struck down: within just two days or so from the onset of the symptoms, the victims died, and no vaccines were able to help them. The strangest thing of all about the disease was that it only harmed individuals belonging to one ethnic group – Navajo Indians (from which the disease got the name 'Navajo syndrome') – and selectively at that: only men of middle height were harmed. As reported by the Russian newspaper *Ezhenedelnaya Gazeta Versia*, Dr Frederick Koster, an epidemiologist from the University of New Mexico, proposed at the time that the deadly disease was caused by a virus which targeted specific genes. It was assumed that such a virus might have been artificially constructed.

And finally, in 1988 in the USSR, a similar disease took several hundred lives in the West Ukrainian town of Chernovtsi. This one infected only children, and seemed to prefer girls of up to 14 years of age with blond hair and blue eyes. The symptoms were absolutely identical to those of 'Navajo syndrome' and modern acute atypical pneumonia, i.e. SARS: a rise in temperature, all the signs of an acute respiratory disease, then hallucinations, a fatal effect on the air passages, and death.

In both the Soviet Union and the USA, these epidemics stopped as suddenly as they had started. No medical, or even logical, reason was ever advanced that could explain the events.

Of course, there is no way to prove that all three cases could have been the result of accidental escapes, or even the planned use, of biological weapons able to 'choose' selectively their victims from within specific areas of the gene pool. And since all development of 'genetic weapons' is forbidden by international conventions, no one ever admits to being involved in research on how to improve them.

A classified 1998 Pentagon report (released to Western journalists only in 2002) says that a biological agent can be genetically modified to create a new and deadly weapon. William Cohen, a former US Secretary of Defense, stated that he had seen reports of work in other countries designed to create 'specific types of pathogens, which could be ethnically specific'.

The Russian newspaper article in *Ezhenedelnaya Gazeta Versia* also referred to a recent report of the British Medical Association, which said that a genetic weapon of mass destruction might be created in as little as ten years. It is therefore possible that, in the not too distant future, the rapid development of genetics might lead to ethnic 'wipe-outs' on a massive scale. The British Medical Association tried to attract worldwide attention to two important circumstances: first, that modern biotechnological research experiments are now carried out in hundred of laboratories, and that in many of them such work is done under extreme secrecy; and second, that the 1972 Biological Weapons Convention doesn't include a system to verify that its provisions are being observed. The situation is becoming more complicated: in developed countries, it is extraordinarily difficult to observe the creation of such weapons because the processes involved can easily be made to seem benign or of purely scientific interest.

Only a lazy investigator of biological weapons fails to mention their appearance in Iraq, despite the fact that until now there has been no single convincing fact or document presented. Ken Alibek writes in *Biohazard* that, in July 1995, Russia opened negotiations with Iraq for the sale of equipment which could have been used for developing and manufacturing bacteriological weapons. 'Negotiations were called off by the time reports of the deal surfaced in the Western press … Many similar deals have gone ahead undetected.'

In 1980 the USA insisted that the only country which had broken the 1972 Biological Weapons Convention was the Soviet Union. By 1995 the list of 'peace-breakers' totalled seventeen countries. Among them were Iraq, Syria, Libya, South Africa, Israel, Egypt, Cuba, Bulgaria, India, Vietnam, South Korea, Iran, China, Taiwan, Japan and the USA. Russia was also on the list, even though the Russian government persisted in saying that its military-biological programme had been stopped. If this were so, why are factories for biological weapon production in Russia still kept fully prepared for action? As Stephen Handelman (co-author of *Biohazard*) pointed out in

May 2003 on the *Liberty Live* programme, 'Military laboratories have remained in a working state and they continue to be out of bounds for foreign inspectors, contradicting the responsibilities in this sphere, undertaken in April 1992 by Yeltsin's government. It promised to put an end to experiments with fatal organisms.' Of course, the Russian military-biological complex was never interested in the country's responsibilities. In 1975 the Soviet Union had ratified the 1972 Biological Weapons Convention, but then, in 1979, 105 people died (according to official figures) in Sverdlovsk as a result of the accidental release of combat-grade bacteria. Only at the end of Gorbachev's reign did Russia admit that the unusual outbreak of infectious disease in Sverdlovsk was inflicted by a strain of anthrax which, ostensibly, accidentally escaped from a secret biological centre. Here we are talking about an unknown, offensive, genetically modified biological wepon, the main purpose of which is to harm people according to their sex-gene, i.e. only adult men; more specifically, the enemy's army. It is suspected that among the combat strains created in Sverdlovsk are Ebola virus, encephalitis and Q fever. Right now, the Russian military establishment openly feels remorse for making the big mistake of allowing international inspectors to investigate the incident because it allowed American inspectors to gather information about the disease's spread in urban conditions. The Russian military leadership has never repeated this mistake. So, for instance, all information about the mysterious epidemic which occurred in Oblivskaya village in 1999 has been thoroughly covered up and has disappeared from accessible sources. All Russian websites with the word 'Oblivskaya' in their title are shut down. It is only known that the infection of 140 people was brought on by the Crimean haemorrhagic-fever virus and resulted in the death of dozens of human beings. The disease itself may be tied in with secret experiments carried out at the Volgograd anti-plague research institute.

In their turn, Russian military experts note that during the last few years biological warfare programmes are being strengthened in the USA. In August 1986 Douglas Feight, Deputy Secretary of Defense for Political Affairs, while making a presentation before the US House of Representatives committee on Intelligence, stated that the Pentagon had changed its opinion on the value of biological weaponry from a military point of view, and that the 1972 Biological Weapons Convention, which forbids such weapons, must be accepted as incomplete and uncertain. During the last few years top US army medical-biological centres – including the US Army Medical Research Institute for Infectious Diseases (USARMIID), the Uniformed Services University of the Health Services (USUHS), the Walter Reed Army Institute of Reserach (WRAIR), and the Naval Medical Research Institute (NAMRI) – have taken part in the cloning of the genes of micro-organisms, among which there are many lethal pathogens of the most dangerous diseases. For example, USARMIID has projects dealing with the cloning and expression of genes which code the synthesis of bacteria that cause anthrax, as well as anti-genes of dengue viruses, Japanese encephalitis, Chikungunya disease, O'Nyong-O'Nyong fever, Ross River fever, Hantan fever, yellow fever, Q fever and others. Research experiments dealing with cloning the genes of rickettsia carrying Japanese river fever (tsutsugamushi disease) and Konori fever, bacillary dysentery, and tropical parasitic invasions are carried out at WRAIR.

Other work relating to the expansion and modernisation of biological warfare research is carried out in the USA. As *Word* magazine for 28 May 1994 had it, the US Department of Defense requested $110 million to build new biological laboratories on the territory of the US Army Edgewood Chemical and Biological Center at Aberdeen Proving Ground, Maryland.

In April 2003, the Russian media agency Interfax reported that strains of Siberian anthrax are being made in large volumes in the USA. Scientists Mark Wheelis, from the University of California, and Malcolm Dando, from the University of Bradford, are also convinced that the USA continues to work on creating cassette bombs with biological payloads such as spores of anthrax. In Professor Dando's opinion, US secret biological laboratories are also trying to manufacture genetically modified strains of the most dangerous pathogens in order to create varieties which cannot be countered by modern antibiotics. In 2003, American mass media discovered that the US Army Medical Laboratory at Dugway in Utah is involved in manufacturing spores of anthrax, which in turn are sent to USARMIID at Fort Detrick, Maryland, for experimental programmes dealing with defence from biological weapons. When their characteristics are examined these spores of anthrax are reminiscent of those which, at the end of 2001, were sent all over America by anonymous terrorists (or 'an anonymous terrorist'?), though they are not identical. Conclusions to be drawn from this information are that, first, the biological attack was organised in the very heart of America, and second, that anthrax is still being manufactured in America, even though programmes for creating biological weapons were officially ended several decades ago.

In 2002, in Geneva, talks resumed on how to defend the world against the threat of biological warfare. Unfortunately, the talks were stalled because American delegates refused to sign off on the new rules of international inspection as provided for in the 1972 Biological Weapons Convention. The Americans insisted that reinforcement of international control procedures over biological laboratories would provoke a wave of industrial espionage between governments and between selected biotechnological and pharmacological companies. It seems the Americans may have something to hide in their laboratories.

Countries accuse each other of breaching the 1972 Biological Weapons Convention while the wheels of the biological war machine continue to spin.

Compared with other weapons of mass destruction, modern biological warfare is more acceptable to governments because it can be quite successfully applied in local conflicts. For example, ampoules with botulinum toxin were found in Chechnya during the first period of the war there, at the end of 1994.

The barriers imposed by the 1972 Biological Weapons Convention are crumbling, and it is evident that advances in biotechnology will soon remove them altogether. I think that the revolutionary achievements in gene-splicing technologies (which can be used to create a new generation of biological weaponry, such as, for example, 'ethnic weapons') make it quite simple to avoid the restrictions of current international agreements on the manufacture of biological weaponry. Existing treaties and agreements have failed to cover such advances, and do not touch upon the so-called 'dual purpose' technologies. These, such as the previously mentioned biotechnologies and experiments with recombinant genomes, can be used for the good of humanity, or its destruction.

In the world of modern molecular-genetic research, it is practically impossible to separate legitimate, peace-orientated work from experiments aimed at perfecting offensive biological weapons. It is impossible to draw a clear-cut boundary and say, this work is for war, and this for the welfare of mankind. At present, no national or international laws exist which can clearly determine between 'bad' and 'good' research because the same gene-splicing technologies which are used in legitimate biotechnological processes are also used to produce biological weapons.

Five or ten years ago a line of demarcation existed between secret army medical labs creating offensive micro-organisms and conventional biotech laboratories producing harmless micro-organisms. Now, with the development of new gene-splicing technologies, that has disappeared. By using 'non-dangerous' biotechnologies, scientists have learnt how to make microbes more deadly than before, and can tailor their characteristics. A small volume of such creations could be used to send hundreds of thousands of people to their deaths.

Only a few short years have passed since the structure of the human genome was entirely decoded in 2001. Now knowledge of the molecular basis of life enables us to construct deadly pathogens which are able to quite specifically affect the human genome, and against which there are no effective vaccines. Modern genetic engineering enables direct modification of bacteria and viral genomes, and it is practically impossible to develop antidotes against all the varieties of hazardous micro-organisms. With the deciphering of the human genetic code, the world is faced with entirely new types of biological weapons – ethnic ones, able to target people on the basis of differences found in their genes, to bring them to a state of slow degradation and then extinction. The birth of such a weapon is only a matter of time. It may even exist already.

Universal biological protection (including vaccines against known forms of more dangerous infections) would cost a minimum of $10 billion. But in addition to the cost there is another problem: identification of the disease. Today, there exists the Biological Integral Detection System (BIDS), which, within thirty minutes, can identify four types of well-known emerging pathogens. However, even this smart and expensive system is unable to identify newly created strains of unknown origin. It would be practically impossible to localise man-made combat infections.

Unlike the technology required to produce atomic and chemical weapons, biotechnologies are very simple and the processes of their 'construction' cannot be thoroughly protected as state secrets. They are published in

158

scientific magazines in minute detail. The first thing that one sees at the beginning of any scientific article about research in the fields of the genetic and molecular biology of micro-organisms, virology or applied industrial microbiology research, is a clear explanation of the method and technological processes of the experiment. As a former career intelligence officer who dealt with biological warfare espionage, I am amazed by this carelessness. Using such information, any experienced and skilled specialist – any molecular biologist or microbiologist with tertiary education – could produce lethal bacteria or viruses in a well-equipped conventional microbiological laboratory. Modern biotechnologies in the possession of terrorists, extremist gangs or even just a rogue biologist-researcher, may bring a lot more damage to the world than a nuclear or chemical war.

I think such information and the results of gene-splicing experiments must be kept secret and be accessible only to responsible researchers whose experiments are controlled by their governments. Do we really have to wait until some terrorist organisation or extremist group takes advantage of this knowledge? Perhaps. There's a Russian proverb which says 'Until lightning strikes, a man won't pray'.

The opportunity for even developed countries to detect and contain emerging infectious diseases is very limited, especially if they are caused by novel pathogens. No country in the world has the capacity to protect public health from such threats. In particular, no public-health service in the world could cope with acts of biological terrorism. Early warning systems that would detect the smallest signs of biological and toxin weapons do not exist. Current disease-outbreak surveillance systems do not allow rapid identification of agents or pathogens of emerging diseases, particularly with respect to potential biological and toxin terrorism or sabotage.

National-security risk-management and emergency-response plans still do not pay enough attention to so-called 'soft' targets, facilities where security is given low priority, which could be potential targets for biological sabotage and acts of terrorism.

Other potential 'soft targets' which might attract modern biological espionage are national and regional microbial typing databases and electronic surveillance systems dealing with the early detection of emerging pathogens and monitoring of potential outbreaks, as well as methods of controlling epidemiological infections, which started to be actively created

159

at the end of the 1990s. These networks, databases and disease-surveillance and -control systems have the capacity to detect and determine strains of dangerous pathogens using modern DNA-based methods, identify and investigate outbreaks quickly, and monitor changes in anti-microbial resistance, as well as responding to the consequences of biological terrorist acts. Among those which are known to me are the authoritative and effectual national and international networks for the early detection of dangerous pathogens: these include PulseNet, used by the Center for Disease Control and Prevention (CDC) in the USA, Canada and more than ten countries in the western Pacific, including Australia, Japan, and Korea; the EnterNet surveillance network, which involves all fifteen European Union countries, plus Switzerland and Norway; and the USA's national anti-microbial resistance monitoring system, NARMS.

To this list of new key targets of biological espionage it is necessary to add analytical molecular diagnostic and research laboratories; universities working on new gene-splicing technologies that might lead to weapons; germ warfare and toxin agent detection technologies; genome and protein strictures electronic databases; and bioterrorism response laboratories. Other targets might include the records of important parameters of modern technological processes, and data from genetic experiments to perfect new biological and pharmacological organisms and products that may lead to the development of biological and toxin weapons, stored in the computer records and databases of private companies and research laboratories.

Not one of these 'soft targets' is categorised as 'secret'. These are not top-secret bunkers, secret command headquarters, ballistic-missile complexes, or even secret biological laboratories. Until recently, security risk management has not been given serious consideration when it comes to protecting stockpiled information for biological and chemical materials. This is why they are very vulnerable to the threat of terrorist acts and biological espionage. To start a panic throughout a whole country there is no need for massive explosions in trade centres or airplane crashes aimed at civilian and military targets. One or two large-scale contaminations of peaceful civilian objectives by pathogens or toxins would be quite enough.

Events since 11 September 2001 have made the whole world aware of and alert to such possibilities. For example, I personally do not exclude the possibility that the cases of inhalation anthrax in the USA at the end of 2001 were used by intelligence agencies (probably of countries outside the USA) to measure the reaction of national governments to the application of biological or toxin warfare, and to gain a clearer picture of emergency plans and means of protection from such a weapon.

In the 1960s it was already being suggested by the Americans that terrorist groups or the world's poorer nations might one day use bacteriological warfare as a weapon. As early as 1959, the Science and Astronautics Committee of the US House of Representatives mentioned that bacteriological warfare was not then competitive with nuclear weapons, but that its real potential lay in the future as 'the poor man's atomic bomb'.

At the end of 2002, the NATO countries created multinational rapid-response teams to mitigate future acts of biological and chemical terrorism. When I thought about the main tasks and methods of these teams, I concluded that they would not be effective for a number of reasons. First of all, the region under their control is restricted to the countries of Western Europe. Another weak link in the chain is the inability to foresee and prevent acts of terrorism. Why? Because the key task of the teams is to respond to attacks and to mitigate their consequences. Their main responsibilities are to collect information on unusual outbreaks of diseases before they get out of control, to assess the effects of terrorist acts already committed, and to advise military commanders on how to deal with them. There is not a word about precautionary measures, nothing about gathering intelligence and counter-terrorist operations! Taking into account mass panic, the shortage or complete lack of appropriate vaccines, and the inability to diagnose offensive combat pathogens quickly, I believe that the effectiveness of these teams in the event of a real attack would not be high.

In 2003, the US government established a new Homeland Security Department. This includes a special division that analyses intelligence from the CIA and FBI in the hope of thwarting future acts of terrorism on American soil. Twenty-two federal agencies including the Secret Service, the Coast Guard and Border Control have been consolidated – completely or partially – under the control of this department, which has about 200,000 employees. The department's consolidated budget is up to $40 billion. It is expected to police almost five million people, more than eleven million trucks, more than 50,000 foreign ships and more than two million rail cars that enter the country each year! Its prime task is to screen out would-be attackers and find biological and toxin weapons.

When signing the Homeland Security Act in November 2002, President George W. Bush said, 'With a vast nation to defend, we can neither predict nor prevent every conceivable attack, and in a free and open society no department of government can completely guarantee our safety.'

Can the task of screening out potential terrorists by the Homeland Security Department and by NATO rapid-response teams be achieved? Is that feasible? Is it possible to achieve the desired result: to detect and to prevent terrorist acts on American territory and in Europe? I do not think so. President Bush's words at the signing of the Homeland Security Act are a clear sign of this.

That is why I believe that only through pre-emptive activities, which should be carried out by intelligence services, can control of biological terrorism be achieved.

The intelligence services of one country, no matter how effective they may be, are not in a position to monitor what goes on everywhere else in the world. At the present time there is a pressing need for co-ordination of activities between all the Western nations and those former Communist Bloc countries that have ever had their own biological weapons pro-grammes. Even countries like Israel and Iraq need to be a part of the solution.

What is more, I think that there is a strong need for an independent, internationally co-operative independent agency for biological security under the auspices of the United Nations, an organisation similar to the International Atomic Energy Agency.

Such an agency should deal with clandestine biological weapons through-out the world and should have the power to enforce the active co-operation of all countries, and all scientists who work in those countries.

The effort that, since 2003, has been applied to the detection of Iraqi biological warfare activities should also be applied to the biological warfare activities (overt and covert) of all other nation states. I consider that the proposed international organisation for biological warfare control – let us call it the International Biological Security Agency – should be prepared to learn from the best practices of its member states. For example, the country in which I now live is characterised by minimal corruption, and it also has a large set of very comprehensive laws covering the management of hazardous substances and organisms. In terms of this body of law no person (and that includes the country's intelligence services) can bring in or manufacture any new hazardous substance or new or novel organisms without prior approval of the relevant state agency (Environmental Risk Management Authority). In addition it has to prove in open public hearings the benefits of its proposal and how any adverse consequences will be properly managed and mitigated. I propose that my new country's system of controlling hazardous substances and hazardous organisms should become the basis of the new international law that our planet desperately needs. This new law should be added to, or perhaps replace, the current poorly worded and unenforceable Biological and Toxin Weapons Convention of 1972.

I realise that private-industry and public-sector research organisations throughout the world stand to be threatened by this development. Under my proposal the risks of patent infringement are considerable. However, by not doing anything there is a greater risk that existing technologies, which have been developed in good faith and with good intent, will become perverted for biological warfare and terrorism.

To be effective the new International Biological Security Agency must have the full support of international science expertise drawn from the existing intelligence agencies – such as the Russian Foreign Intelligence Service, plus Russia's GRU, China's GRI, the CIA, MI6, Germany's BND, France's SDECE, Israel's Mossad, and the intelligence services of other countries. The active co-operation of all intelligence agencies is necessary to ensure that all possible future technological developments are assessed in terms of both their potential for good and their potential for harm. One such example is research into the genomes of emerging pathogens and related human health issues. This research must be closely monitored to ensure that the risk of new weapons being developed in secret is minimised.

I think that a necessity has emerged for an international law that would define personal liability for the results of molecular-genetic experiments. This liability must be borne equally by the research scientist who produces new genetically modified organisms, and by the officials of the central government bodies who are responsible for the final decision to manufacture and use the organisms created in the research laboratory. In one of my articles I have already stated that acknowledging personal responsibility for the consequences of genetic experimentation should become one of the elements of a new code of conduct for microbiologists and geneticists. Within the framework of the new international law, an expert council from industry and academia might be established to spot evolving areas of risk in the biological sciences while using final products of their research. Some restrictions might be also imposed.

I believe that, because of the possibility of biological terrorism, governments should, as part of their homeland security procedures, review their national services and programmes dealing with diagnostic and disease prevention policies. It is necessary to unite all existing national microbial-typing databases and electronic surveillance systems dealing with control, detection and recognition of emergent diseases into one global net under, for example, the new International Biological Security Agency or the World Health Organisation. This global net should help share data and information, predict sudden potential disease outbreaks for one or the other part of the planet, control pathogen surveillance and monitor changes, identify potential pathogens by strain level, conduct epidemiological investigations and assess inevitable losses. Obviously the independent, uncoordinated, national and international systems and databases must be reliably secured against unauthorised access and clandestine penetration. I think that the establishment of such a global network for emergent and warfare-agent infections, which would allow timely detection and identification of threats to national security in participating countries, should be one of the first and most important goals in the creation of an effective multinational biological security system.

A modern war does not have to start with the application of 'traditional', i.e. conventional, means of mass destruction, including atomic weapons. To prepare secretly and initiate a biological war is quite possible even under conditions of rigid international control. It is quite enough to have a few up-to-date and well-equipped covert biological laboratories, well-trained fighters and terrorists, and effective intelligence services.

After having read my book, people may wonder what the world is coming to. However, they should take heart: while the threat is real, the climate for international co-operation has never been better. A world community of science and scientists now exists where previously there was only rivalry. Added to this, the threat of international terrorism has pushed countries that previously were enemies into active co-operation and partnership.

In the end, we all live on one planet, under the same sky. Provided we all act sensibly and rationally, I believe the twenty-first century should still be a good time to live.

Appendix A

The Structure of Directorate S (Special Operations) in 1984–92

Head of Directorate S
Four deputies of the head of Directorate S

Group R
Intelligence information analytical group under the personal supervision of the head of Directorate S.

Secretariat
Processing of routine day-to-day flow of secret correspondence of Directorate S's operational departments with the Foreign Intelligence Service's *rezidenturas* in target countries, directorates of the Foreign Intelligence Service and other Russian intelligence and counter-intelligence communities, and with the Russian central government and the Presidential Council.

Department 1 (Special Reserve)
The most secret operations and important tasks are carried out by the highly experienced former 'Illegals' – career intelligence professionals – of the 'Special Reserve' by order of the heads of the Foreign Intelligence Service and the leaders of the country.

APPENDIX A

Department 2
Selection, acquisition and processing of documents, cover documentation, and bogus life stories for Illegals.

Department 3
Selection, training and deployment of Illegals in target countries.

Department 4
Special operations in the United States, Canada and Latin America.

Department 5
Special operations in Western Europe.

Department 6
Special operations in China, Japan, South-East Asia and the Pacific rim countries. Disbanded in 1991, when its functions were transferred to other departments of Directorate S.

Department 7
Special operations in the Arabic-speaking North African countries, countries of the Near and Middle East, and on the Indian subcontinent.

Department 8
Training of deep-cover officers (Illegals) and fighters for carrying out terror attacks, acts of sabotage and diversions. Responsible for planning, preparing and carrying out acts of terrorism and sabotage in the event of a large-scale military conflict and war. In 1992, Department 8 was amalgamated with Department 12. The new department was called Department 8 but its head was the former head of Department 12.

Department 9
Deals with the security of special operations carried out by Directorate S's Illegals.

Department 10

Cultivation and recruitment of foreign citizens on the territory of the Soviet Union – now Russia – and controlling them in target countries.

Department 11

Support of special operations by operational techniques and electronic surveillance.

Department 12

International biological espionage and special operations. In 1992, Department 12 was amalgamated with Department 8. The new department was named Department 8 but its head was the former head of the old Department 12.

Department 13

Provides security and the cover stories for Directorate S's conspiracy apartments in Moscow and overseas. Provides support for Illegals and especially valuable agents during their recalls to Moscow or other places for debriefs. Dismantled in 1991, Department 13's functions were transferred to other operational departments of Directorate S.

Appendix B

The Structure of Department 12
(Amalgamated with Department 8 in 1992)

Head of Department 12
Deputy head of Department 12
Secretariat

The First, American, Section
United States, Canada and Latin American countries.

The Second, European, Section
All Western European countries, including NATO and allied countries, plus the English- and French-speaking countries of Africa.

The Third, Eastern, Section
Countries of the Near and Middle East, South-East Asia and the Pacific rim countries (including Australia, New Zealand, China and Japan).

Commercial Section
Dealt with Department 12's operations carried out under novel commercial covers in target countries.

Sabotage and Diversion Section
Established in 1992 after Department 12's consolidation with Department 8, this section dealt with planning and preparing acts of sabotage and diversion in target countries.

Covers Group
Officers carrying out Department 12's tasks in target countries under academic and administrative cover, i.e. by posing as genuine research scientists and as officials of various Russian state and government organisations, commissions, representatives of various international organisations, commissions and research centres dealing with public and animal health, ecological, environmental, biotechnological issues, etc.

Staging and Deployment Group
Dealt with staging – the first short-term overseas training assignments of new Illegals – and their final deployment in target countries.

Appendix C

The Main Targets of Department 12
(List based on the author's personal recollections*)

The USA

US Armed Forces Establishments
The US Army Chemical and Biological Defense Command
The Biological Defense Research Directorate
The US Defense Department
The US Arms Control and Disarmament Agency
The US Army Medical Research Institute for Infectious Diseases
  (USARMIID) at Fort Detrick, Maryland
The US Army Edgewood Chemical and Biological Center at Aberdeen
  Proving Ground, Maryland
The US Army Center for Health Promotion and Preventive Medicine at
  Aberdeen Proving Ground, Maryland
The US Army vaccine and research laboratories, New Mexico
The US Army's Dugway Proving Ground in Utah and the Battelle
  company in Ohio
The Armed Forces Institute of Pathology in Washington, DC

---

* This is only a small sample based on my recollection of those objectives in target countries that
Department 12 was interested in. A complete list of the targets of Department 12 included several
hundred 'objectives of interest', located in practically all of the developed countries of the world.

The Naval Medical Research Center, Bethesda, Maryland
Wright-Patterson Air Force Base, near Dayton, Ohio

US Non-Military Establishments
The US Departments of Health and Agriculture
The US National Research Council
The National Center for Infectious Disease, Center for Disease Control
    and Prevention, Maryland, Atlanta
The Institute for Genomic Research, Maryland
The Centers for Disease Control and Prevention's Division of Vector-
    Borne Infectious Diseases, Fort Collins, Colorado
The National Institutes of Health, Bethesda, Maryland
The US National Academy of Sciences Institute of Medicine
The Center for Complex Infectious Diseases in Rosemead, California
The Center for Adaptation Genetics and Drug Resistance at Tufts
    University, Boston
The US National Cancer Institute, Washington, DC
The US National Human Genome Research Institute, Washington, DC
The US Department of Energy's Lawrence Livermore National and Los
    Alamos Laboratories
Cold Spring Harbor Laboratory, New York
Massachusetts Institute of Technology
The John Hopkins Center for Civilian Biodefense Studies, John Hopkins
    University, Baltimore
The US National Institutes of Health's collection of publicly available
    DNA sequences
The Center for Complex Infectious Disease in Rosemead, California
The US Agency for Toxic Substances and Disease Registry
The US Type Culture Collection in Rockville, Maryland

Canada
The Suffield Biodefence Laboratory, Alberta

Britain
The UK Chemical and Biological Defence Establishment (laboratories) at
    Porton Down near Salisbury
The British Government's Defence Evaluation and Research Agency
PHLS Communicable Disease Surveillance Centre, London
The Centre for Applied Microbiology and Research at Porton Down
The London School of Hygiene and Tropical Medicine
The Scottish Centre for Infection and Environmental Health in Glasgow
The University of Oxford

France
The French National Agency for Research on AIDS
Pasteur Research Centres

Germany
Max Planck Institute in Göttingen
Hoechst AG in Wiesbaden, and affiliated companies

Israel
Weizmann Institute of Science in Rehovot
The Hebrew University of Jerusalem

Multinational International Agencies and Companies
NATO headquarters in Brussels, Belgium
World Health Organisation headquarters in Geneva, Switzerland
Food and Agriculture Organisation headquarters in Rome, Italy
United Nations special commissions dealing with biological programmes
Biotechnological, pharmaceutical and DNA discovery companies, includ-
    ing Ciba-Geigy, DuPont, Johnson and Johnson, Merck, Monsanto,
    etc., and their affiliated companies mainly in the USA, Britain, France,
    Germany, Belgium, Switzerland and Sweden

APPENDIX C

Targets common to all Department 12's target countries, including the NATO countries and their allies

Army Medical (Biological) Research Laboratories and Centres
Armed forces medical and biodefence laboratories dealing with
   experiments with dangerous pathogens, re-emerging infectious diseases
   and means against biological and toxin warfare
BSL3 and BSL4 containment facilities and laboratories with biosafety level
   3 or 4, working with dangerous pathogens
Laboratories and research centres holding strains of biological dangerous
   or warfare pathogens, anticrop and antilivestock weapons and also
   vaccines and antidotes against them
Biological and toxin warfare munitions stockpiles

State and Private Sector
Central government, defence departments, directorates and services dealing
   with emergency situations and response planning, pandemic preparedness
   plans, programmes of protection against biological and toxin weapons,
   surveillance programmes regarding prevention of potential acts of
   biological sabotage and terrorism and liquidation of their consequences,
   development of means of protection from biological weapons, control
   of the most dangerous epidemiological diseases, public health and
   biosecurity issues, etc.
Biotechnological and pharmaceutical private companies dealing with the
   development of a vast range of novel drugs and vaccines, and the
   development of preventive measures and treatment against the most
   dangerous pathogens of human beings, animals and plants
Vaccine research laboratories and factories

Other Public Sector Organisations
Legitimate genomics and pharmacological research laboratories,
   institutes, and centres dealing with gene-splicing technologies and
   their military implications, and genetic experiments with dangerous
   pathogens and novel organisms with specific and planned
   characteristics

175

Disease outbreak and laboratory surveillance systems dealing with early detection of emerging pathogens, the monitoring of potential outbreaks, and methods of control of epidemiological infections

Research laboratories, institutes and centres dealing with genome data work and using unknown genes which have been linked to specific diseases, and with developing genetically altered pathogens resistant to antibodies and vaccines

Collections of genetic variants of dangerous pathogens and their DNA sequences, including microbial genome databases

Facilities with stocks of dangerous virus cultures, repositories with new drugs and vaccines

Early warning of a biological toxin weapons attack systems and detectors

Appendix D

Organisation of the KGB First Chief Directorate and the Russian Foreign Intelligence Service (SVR)

KGB First Chief Directorate

Director
Deputy Directors
Secretarial and Personnel Section

Directorates

Directorate P	*Political Intelligence*
Department 1	USA, Canada
Department 2	Latin America
Department 3	United Kingdom, Australia, Africa, New Zealand, Scandinavia
Department 4	Eastern Europe, Western Germany, Austria
Department 5	Belgium, Netherlands, Dania, Luxembourg, France, Spain, Portugal, Switzerland, Greece, Italy, Yugoslavia, Albania, Romania
Department 6	China, Vietnam, Laos, Cambodia, North Korea
Department 7	Thailand, Indonesia, Japan, Malaysia, Singapore, Philippines
Department 8	Non-Arabic-speaking Near East countries, including Afghanistan, Iran, Israel, Turkey
Department 9	Anglophone countries of Africa

Department 10   Francophone countries of Africa
Department 11   Liaison with Socialist countries
Department 12   Registration and archives
Department 13   Electronic interception and operations against
                 cryptographical agencies of Western intelligence services
Department 14   India, Sri-Lanka, Pakistan, Nepal, Bangladesh, Burma
Department 15   Arabic-speaking countries of the Near East, and Egypt
Department 16   Immigration
Department 17   Liaison with developing countries

Directorate S   *Illegal Intelligence*
Directorate T   Scientific and Technical Intelligence
Directorate K   External Counter-Intelligence
Directorate OT   Operational and Technical Support
Directorate R   Operational Planning and Analysis
Directorate I   Computer Service (Information Dissemination)
Directorate RT   Operations within the Soviet Union

Services

Service A: Disinformation (Secret Operations)
Service R: Radio Communications with Overseas Residencies
Service A of Directorate 8: Cryptographical Services

Institutes

Institute of Intelligence Information
Andropov Red Banner Intelligence Institute

Russian Foreign Intelligence Service (SVR)

Director
Deputy Directors
Secretarial and Personnel Section
Communications (Public and Mass Media) Section

Directorates

Directorate P   Political Intelligence
Directorate S   Illegal Intelligence
Directorate T   Scientific and Technical Intelligence
Directorate K   External Counter-Intelligence
Directorate OT Operational and Technical Support
Directorate R   Operational Planning and Analysis
Directorate I   Computer Service (Information Dissemination)
Directorate of Economic Intelligence

Services

Service R: Radio Communications with Overseas Residencies
Service A of Directorate 8: Cryptographical Services

Institutes

Institute of Intelligence Information
Andropov Red Banner Intelligence Academy

Select Bibliography

Alibek, Ken, with Stephen Handelman, *Biohazard: The Chilling True Story of the Largest Covert Biological Weapons Program in the World Told from the Inside by the Man Who Ran It*, London, 1999

Drozdov, Yuri, *Zapiski Nachalnika Nelegalnoi Razvedki* [*Memoirs of the Head of Illegal Intelligence*], Moscow, 2000

Kuzichkin, Vladimir, *Inside the KGB: Myth and Reality*, trans. Thomas B. Beattie, London, 1990

Sudoplatov, Pavel, and Anatoli Sudoplatov et al., *Special Tasks: The Memoirs of an Unwanted Witness – A Soviet Spymaster*, London, 1994

West, Nigel, *The Illegals: The Double Lives of the Cold War's Most Secret Agents*, London, 1993

Glossary

Agar. A gelatinous culture medium made from certain seaweeds and used for preserving and growing of bacterial cultures.

Biopreparat. The Soviet Union–Russian biological weapons programme's agency.

BND. (West) German Intelligence Service.

Bundeswehr. The (West) German army.

Centre, or Service. The headquarters of the Russian Foreign Intelligence Service, located in Yasenevo, Moscow's south-west suburb.

Cheka. All-Russian Extraordinary Commission for Combating Counter-revolution and Sabotage (the predecessor of KGB) (1917–22).

Chekist. Secret official of Bolshevik Cheka. FSB and FIS officers in the 1990s (and even now) still styled themselves Chekists in honour of the first Soviet security and intelligence agency – the Cheka, or Chrezvychaynaya Komissiya, which was founded by Lenin on 20 December 1917.

CIA. Central Intelligence Agency (USA).

Department 12. An operational department of Directorate S of the KGB's First Chief Directorate – the department for the conduct of international biological espionage (intelligence) activities, and for the planning and preparation of acts of biological sabotage and terrorism in target countries in the event of war.

Directorate K. The External Counter-Intelligence Directorate of the KGB's First Chief Directorate.

Directorate S, or the Illegals Directorate. The inner core of the KGB's First Chief Directorate. Responsible for co-ordinating the activities of Russian intelligence operatives, who spy under assumed names and professions in target countries. They are referred to in KGB–FIS circles as 'Illegals'.

Directorate T. The Scientific Technical Intelligence Directorate of the KGB's First Chief Directorate.

FBI. The Federal Bureau of Investigation, i.e. the USA's domestic security and anti-crime agency.

First Chief Directorate. The foreign intelligence of the KGB, since 1991 renamed as the Russian Foreign Intelligence Service (the FIS) and more recently the External Intelligence Service (SVR).

FIS. The re-created Russian Foreign Intelligence Service, or (as it is now known) the SVR – the successor to the KGB's First Chief Directorate, it is the Russian equivalent of Britain's MI6 and the USA's CIA.

FSB. The newly created Russian Counter-Intelligence Service, the Russian equivalent of Britain's MI5 and the USA's FBI.

FSK. The Russian Counter-Intelligence Service, successor to the KGB's Second Chief Directorate (internal counter-intelligence), the predecessor of the FSB.

Glavmikrobioprom, or Bioprom. The Soviet and Russian Chief Agency of the Microbiological Industry.

GRI. Chinese Intelligence Service.

GRU. Chief Intelligence Directorate – Soviet (and Russian) Military Intelligence Service.

IAEA. The International Atomic Energy Agency.

Illegals. Russian (and Soviet) intelligence operatives, secretly deployed abroad and operating covertly under assumed names and life stories. They masquerade as citizens of target or Western countries.

KGB. Committee of State Security (Soviet secret police).

KI. The KGB's Andropov Red Banner Intelligence Institute of the First Chief Directorate. Now named an academy. The institute trained people who were recruited to work as career intelligence officers of the Russian Foreign Intelligence Service.

'Kukushka', or 'cuckoo'. A conspiracy apartment (KGB jargon).

Line N. A unit of a KGB (Russian Foreign Intelligence Service) overseas residency which supports operations of Illegals in the target country.

Line N Support officer. An intelligence officer of the Line N of the KGB and the Russian Foreign Intelligence Service overseas residency.

MI5. British Security Service – for internal security.

MI6. British Secret Intelligence Service (a.k.a. SIS) – for external intelligence gathering and counter-Intelligence work.

Mossad. Israeli Secret Intelligence Service.

NIIRP. The First Chief Directorate's Scientific-Research Institute for Intelligence Problems (*Nauchno-Issledovatelskii Institut Razvedivatelnikh Problem*).

NIS, or the Newly Independent States. Former republics of the Soviet Union, which, after disintegration of the Soviet Union in 1991, became independent states.

Politburo. The ruling body of both the Communist Party and the Soviet Union.

Rezident. Fixed-post spy, the chief of the 'Illegal' network in the target country.

Rezidenturas. Soviet (and Russian) Foreign Intelligence Service stations located within Soviet and Russian embassies and trade delegations in target countries.

Run-in. A short-term overseas training assignment, or a staging, of an 'Illegal'.

SDECE. French Secret Intelligence Service.

Second Chief Directorate. The former KGB internal counter-intelligence directorate, now the FSB.

Special agents. Nationals of foreign countries who were recruited by the Russian Foreign Intelligence Service to spy on their own home countries. They got extensive operational and intelligence training, and were provided with necessary equipment. In some instances these were people already working in research institutes and laboratories in their home countries. Special agents were willing to betray to Department 12 secrets associated with their work.

Stasi. East German Ministry of State Security.

SVR. The re-created Russian Foreign Intelligence Service (the FIS), the Russian equivalent of the British MI6 and the USA's CIA. From *Sluzhba Vneshnei Razvedki.*

Undercovers. Career intelligence officers of Department 12 of Directorate S who operate under various guises, i.e. they use the academic, research and administrative cover of legitimate scientific research institutes of the Russian Academy of Sciences, of state or government organisations and of representatives of various international organisations and commissions dealing with public health, environmental, ecological and other medical and biological fields.

Villa. The training centre of the Russian Foreign Intelligence Service, the Andropov Red Banner Intelligence Institute (Academy).

VOLNA. Department 12's channel of expedited international delivery of live biological materials from target countries via Moscow's international airport for subsequent delivery to Russian secret medical and biological research laboratories and centres controlled by the Russian Foreign Intelligence Service.

Index

187

Sukhoi, 145
Sverdlovsk, 155
SVR, *see* Russian Foreign Intelligence Service
Sweden, 38, 94
Switzerland, 160
Syria, 4

Taiwan, 154
Tajikistan, 66
Tarusov, Professor Boris, 41
TASS, 38
Tehran, 69
terrorism, *see* biological terrorism
Thailand, 123
Toronto, 116
toxins, 38
TREFY, 38, 89, 91–3
Tsuryupa, Colonel Victor, 47
tularaemia, 26, 101; American strain, 32
Turkey, 38, 79, 120

Uniformed Services University of the Health
  Services (USUHS), 156
United Nations, 162
United States of America, 14, 33, 38, 47, 154;
  as target of American Section, Department
  12, 54–5, 57, 99–101; DACHNIKI atomic
  secrets, 26; KGB stations in, 79; remains
  target after 1991, 135; terminate biological
  weapons development, 151
US Army Medical Laboratory, Dugway, 156
US Army Medical Research Institute for
  Infectious Diseases (USARMIID), *see* Fort
  Detrick
US Defense Department, 82, 156
Ustinov, Dr, 32n
Uzbekistan, 133

V., Major Dmitri, 134
vaccines, 38, 67, 73–4, 83–4, 137–8, 151;
  shortage of, 161; universal biological
  protection, 158; in USA, 101; in West
  Germany, 92

Varenik, Major Gennady, 64, 84; psychotropic
  drugs in interrogation of, 107
VASILIEV (head of Department 12), 74
Vienna, 58, 91, 135
Vietnam, 139, 154
VILE (Oleg Gordievsky), 58
viruses, 76, 83; genome modification, 158;
  research in France, 95; from USA, 99–102
Volgograd, 76; anti-plague research institute in,
  155; West Nile fever in, 150
VOLNA, 73; author delivers packages, 74–7;
  auxiliary channel, 139; dangers of, 78;
  emeralds sent by, 143; growth of, after 1991,
  135; materials from USA, 100
Vorobiev hills, 98
Vorobyov, General Anatoly, 28

Walter Reed Army Institute of Research
  (WRAIR), 156
War of Wits (Ladislas Farago), 23
Washington DC, 14, 79, 111
West Nile fever, 150
Wheelis, Mark, 156
World Health Organisation (WHO), 38, 66–7,
  164

Y., Colonel Vladimir, 143
YAN, 84, 97–9
yellow fever, 156
Yeltsin, Boris, 147, 155
Yershinia, 101
Yurchenko, Colonel Vitaly, 107
Yuzbashyan, Colonel, 141
YURI, 104

Zaire, 46n
Zhuravlev, General Yuri, 119